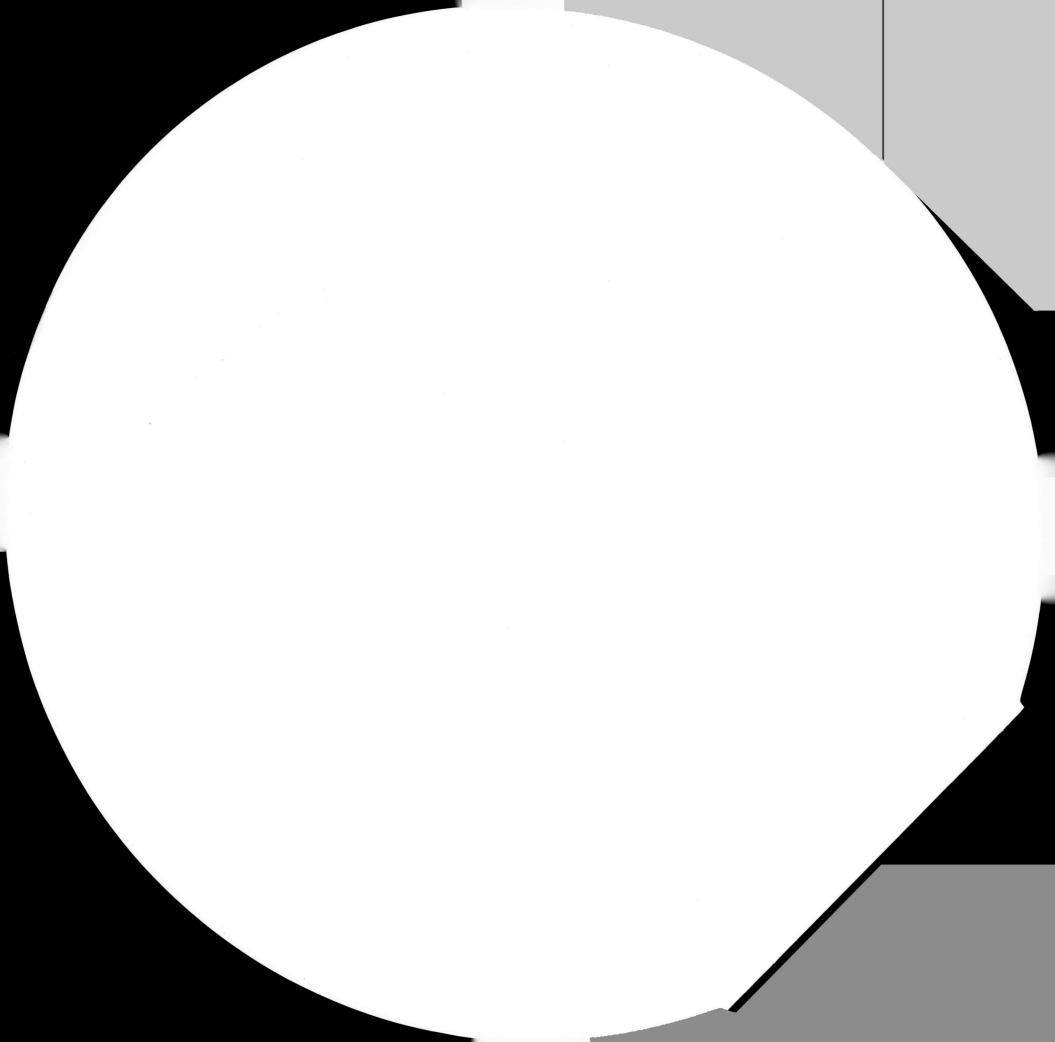

PASTA

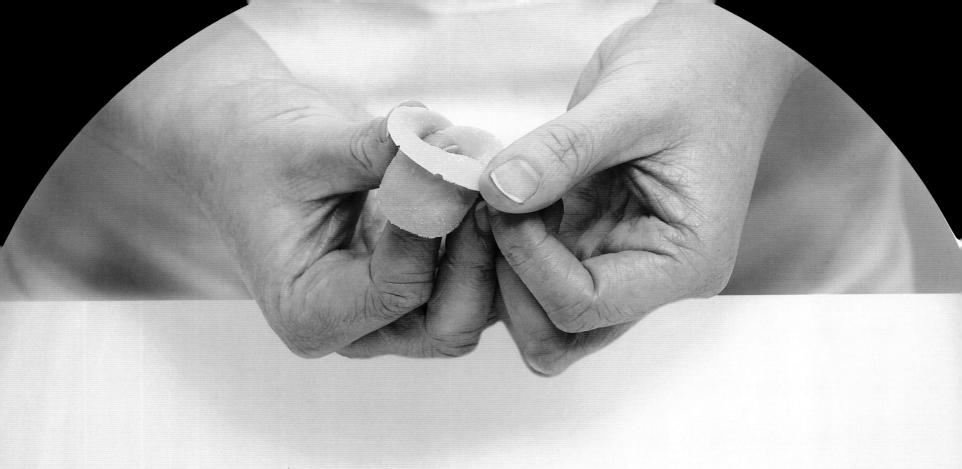

This book was conceived, edited and designed by
McRae Publishing Ltd, London
www.mcraepublishing.co.uk

Publishers Anne McRae, Marco Nardi

Project Director Anne McRae
Art Director Marco Nardi
Photography Brent Parker Jones
Text Carla Bardi
Editing Alison Price, Daphne Trotter
Food Styling Lee Blaylock
Layouts Aurora Granata
Prepress Filippo Delle Monache

ISBN 978-1-910122-19-8

Printed in China

PASTA

CARLA BARDI

mc
rae
PUBLISHING

MORE THAN 55 DELICIOUS RECIPES FOR PASTA LOVERS

healthy pasta
meals

Pasta is the cornerstone of the healthy Mediterranean diet. Cholesterol-free and very low in sodium, pasta delivers the slow-releasing complex carbohydrates we need to power us through the day. It is served bathed in nutrient-rich sauces based on anti-oxident tomatoes, fiber-filled vegetables and beans, heart-healthy olive oil and fish, poultry, and meats.

Current dietary guidelines suggest that around 60 percent of our daily calorie intake should come from carbohydrates, making pasta an ideal choice. Pasta has a low glycemic index, which means that it doesn't cause unhealthy spikes in blood sugar levels and, if you prefer to avoid refined carbohydrates, it is readily available in a range of whole-wheat (wholemeal) varieties.

But pasta is more than just a healthy food; as our recipes will show, it is also delicious, versatile, and widely admired. You can serve it to people of all ages and on any occasion: small children will gobble up linguine in a simple tomato sauce (literally, with their hands; see page 14); vegetarians will happily eat a bowl of whole-wheat pasta with grilled veggies (see page 36); while gourmet food-lovers will be thrilled with fresh watercress tagliolini with lemon & dill sauce (see page 104). We have also included a host of classic dishes, from bucatini all'amatriciana (see page 20) and spaghetti with meatballs (see page 74) to tagliatelle with Bolognese meat sauce (see page 94), and classic lasagna (see page 116). Buon appetito!

Plain fresh pasta is made of a simple mixture of flour and eggs.

2²/3 cups (400 g) all-purpose (plain) flour
• 4 very fresh large eggs

SERVES 4 • **PREPARATION** 30 MINUTES + TME TO REST

fresh pasta dough

 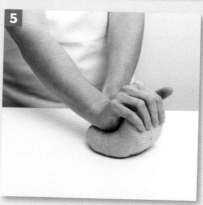 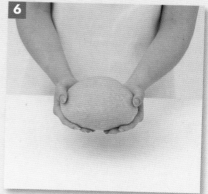

1. Sift the flour onto a clean work surface and shape into a mound. Make a hollow in the center.

2. Use a fork to beat the eggs lightly in a small bowl. Pour the beaten eggs into the center of the mound of flour.

3. Use the fork to mix the eggs into the flour. Take care not to break the outer wall of flour or the eggs will run.

4. When almost all the flour has been absorbed, use your hands and a pasta scraper (if you have one) to gather the dough into a ball.

5. Knead on a lightly floured work surface by pushing down and forward on the pasta with the heel of your palm. Fold in half, give a quarter-turn, and repeat.

6. After 10–15 minutes, it will be smooth and silky, with tiny air bubbles on the surface. Let rest for 30 minutes.

rolling & cutting
fresh pasta dough
BY MACHINE

Fresh ribbon pasta types are named according to their width. The narrowest ribbons, taglierini or tagliolini, are about ¼ inch (5–6 mm) wide. Tagliatelle (also known as fettuccine) are normally about ½ inch (1 cm) wide, while pappardelle can be up to 1 inch (2.5 cm) wide.

1. **Divide** the dough into six equal pieces (for 14 ounces or 400 g of pasta, enough for four people).

2. **Roll** a piece of dough at the thickest setting. Continue rolling, reducing the thickness setting one notch at a time.

3. **The sheets** should be evenly shaped. Long sheets are hard to manage; don't make them any longer than 12–14 inches (30–35 cm).

4. **Dust** the sheets with flour or semolina and cover with a clean dry cloth. Let dry a little before you begin to cut them.

5. **Test** to see if ready to cut: insert your index finger into a fold of pasta and pull slightly. If it tears, it is ready. Set the machine to the width required and run each sheet through. Gather the pasta up and shape into "nests."

6. **Set** the machine to the width required and run each sheet through. Gather the pasta up and shape into "nests."

Ravioli can be round, square, rectangular, or triangular in shape. Fillings can be made with meat, seafood, cheese or vegetables. Do not roll the pasta sheets too thin; roll to the second thinnest setting on your machine. The pasta needs to be strong enough to hold the filling.

preparing
ravioli

1

1. Prepare the pasta dough and roll out into thin sheets. Place teaspoons or balls of filling in rows 2 inches (5 cm) apart on half of each pasta sheet. Fold the other half of each sheet over the top.

2

2. Press down gently between the blobs of filling with your fingertips to remove the air. Use a plain or fluted pastry cutter or cookie cutter to cut out disks. Re-roll the scraps and repeat until all the filling and pasta are used.

3

3. You can make the ravioli any size you like. They can have smooth or fluted edges. You can also make square ravioli by simply cutting between the blobs on the filled pasta sheets with a knife or pasta wheel.

preparing half-moon
ravioli & tortellini

Use a round pastry or cookie cutter to make half-moon-shaped ravioli. With just a little extra folding these can become exquisite little tortellini ("little cakes") or slightly larger tortelloni. Tortelloni can be so large that you only need to serve 3 or 4 per person.

1. Roll the pasta into sheets on a floured work surface. Use a smooth 3-inch (8-cm) pastry or cookie cutter to cut out disks of pasta.

2. Shape heaped teaspoons of filling in balls. Put one at the center of each disk.

3. Fold the pasta over to seal in a half-moon shape.

4. To prepare tortellini, continue by folding the edges of the half-moon pasta back on themselves. Finish by twisting the pasta around your index finger and sealing the ends together.

5. Slide the tortelloni off your finger.

6. You can make large tortelloni, by using a larger cutter for the disks and more filling.

potato **gnocchi**

SERVES 6 · PREPARATION 45 MINUTES + 1–2 HOURS TO REST · COOKING 30–35 MINUTES

2 pounds (1 kg) potatoes, with peel · 1²/₃ cups (250 g) all-purpose (plain) flour · ½ teaspoon salt · 1 large egg, lightly beaten · 3 tablespoons freshly grated Parmesan cheese

1. **Boil** the potatoes in a pot of salted water until tender, 20–25 minutes. Drain well and let cool a little. Scrape the skins off while still warm.

2. **Mix in** the flour, salt, egg, and Parmesan and stir until well mixed. Mash until smooth in a bowl.

3. **Shape** the gnocchi dough into a ball. Break off pieces and roll them into cylinders just slightly thicker than your index finger. Cut into pieces about 1 inch (2.5 cm) long. Let dry for 1–2 hours on a clean cloth dusted with flour or semolina.

4. **To make ridged gnocchi** (which hold sauces better), roll the gnocchi one by one around the tines of a fork.

5. **Cook** the gnocchi in batches in a large pot of salted boiling water until they rise to the surface, 2–3 minutes. Scoop out with a slotted spoon.

10

The sheets of pasta for lasagna have to be blanched for a few seconds in boiling water, then cooled in cold water and gently squeezed. Blanch the sheets in 3 quarts (3 liters) of boiling water with 1 tablespoon of coarse sea salt and 1 tablespoon of olive oil. Cool in the same quantity of cold water, salt, and oil.

preparing & blanching
lasagna sheets

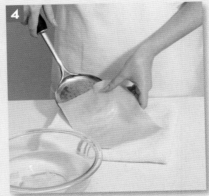

1. Roll each piece of dough through the pasta machine down to the second thinnest setting. Cut into 6 x 8-inch (15 x 20-cm) rectangles.

2. Bring a large pot of water to a boil. Add 1 tablespoon of sea salt and 1 tablespoon of olive oil. Blanch the sheets of pasta one at a time for 3–5 seconds. Remove with a slotted spoon.

3. Prepare a large bowl of cold water with 1 tablespoon each of sea salt and olive oil. Dip each sheet of lasagna into the bowl of cold water, then remove.

4. Squeeze the excess water gently from each sheet. Lay the sheets out in a single layer on a damp cloth.

spaghetti with garlic, chile & oil

PASTA

1 pound (500 g) spaghetti

SAUCE

½ cup (120 ml) extra-virgin olive oil · 6 cloves garlic, finely chopped

2-3 dried chiles, crumbled · 3-4 tablespoons finely chopped fresh parsley

Freshly ground black pepper

SERVES 4-6 · **PREPARATION** 10 MINUTES · **COOKING** 12-15 MINUTES

PASTA **1. Place** a large pot of salted water over high heat and bring to a boil. Cook the pasta in the boiling water until al dente, 10-12 minutes. SAUCE **2. Heat** the oil in a large frying pan over medium heat. Add the chiles and garlic and sauté until the garlic is pale gold, 3-4 minutes.

3. Drain the pasta and add to the frying pan. Sprinkle with the parsley and toss over medium heat for 1-2 minutes. **4. Garnish** with plenty of freshly ground black pepper. **5. Serve** hot.

This is a classic pasta sauce and a favorite for unexpected guests and midnight snacks. A night on the town for a group of Italian students will often end up at someone's apartment with a bowl of steaming, spicy spaghetti.

• **If you liked this recipe, try the spaghetti alla puttanesca on page 24.**

linguine with tomatoes & lemon

PASTA
1 pound (500 g) linguine

SAUCE
2 pounds (1 kg) ripe tomatoes · 4 tablespoons finely chopped fresh basil · 1/3 cup (90 ml) extra-virgin olive oil · Freshly squeezed juice of 1 lemon
2 cloves garlic, finely chopped · Salt and freshly ground black pepper

SERVES 4–6 · **PREPARATION** 15 MINUTES · **COOKING** 10–12 MINUTES

PASTA **1. Place** a large pot of salted water over high heat and bring to a boil. Cook the pasta in the boiling water until al dente, 10–12 minutes. SAUCE **2. Blanch** the tomatoes in boiling water for 2 minutes. Drain and peel them. Chop coarsely and place in a bowl with the basil, oil, lemon juice, and garlic. Season with salt and pepper. **3. Drain** the pasta well and transfer to a large heated serving dish. **4. Add** the tomato mixture and toss well. **5. Serve** hot.

This is a quick and refreshing sauce which is perfect in the summer months when tomatoes are tasty and abundant.

● If you liked this recipe, try the penne with tomatoes & mozzarella on page 16.

14

penne with
tomatoes & mozzarella

PASTA

1 pound (500 g) penne

SAUCE

24 cherry tomatoes, halved · 8 ounces (250 g) fresh mozzarella, drained and cut into small cubes · 2 tablespoons finely chopped fresh basil · 1 tablespoon finely chopped fresh mint · 1 clove garlic, finely chopped · 2 tablespoons extra-virgin olive oil · Salt and freshly ground black pepper

SERVES 4–6 · PREPARATION 15 MINUTES · COOKING 10–12 MINUTES

PASTA 1. Place a large pot of salted water over high heat and bring to a boil. Cook the pasta in the boiling water until al dente, 10–12 minutes. **SAUCE 2. Combine** the cherry tomatoes, mozzarella, basil, mint, garlic, and oil in a medium bowl.

Season with salt and pepper and toss gently. **3. Drain** the pasta well and transfer to a large heated serving bowl. **4. Add** the cherry tomato mixture to the bowl and toss well. **5. Serve** hot.

Make this dish with a high-quality mozzarella made with imported Italian water buffalo cheese. If you can't get a good mozzarella, you can replace it with feta or another cheese of your choice.

• **If you liked this recipe, try the tagliatelle caprese on page 88.**

16

bucatini alla carbonara

PASTA

1 pound (500 g) bucatini

SAUCE

¼ cup (60 ml) extra-virgin olive oil • 1 small onion, finely chopped
5 ounces (150 g) diced bacon • 4–6 large eggs • ⅓ cup (90 ml) heavy (double)
cream • Salt and freshly ground black pepper • ½ cup (60 g) freshly grated pecorino
or Parmesan cheese + extra, to serve

SERVES 4–6 • **PREPARATION** 15 MINUTES • **COOKING** 10–12 MINUTES

PASTA 1. Place a large pot of salted water over high heat and bring to a boil. Cook the pasta in the boiling water until al dente, 10–12 minutes.
SAUCE 2. Heat the oil in a small saucepan over medium heat. Add the onion and sauté until softened, 3–4 minutes. **3. Add** the bacon and sauté until crisp, about 5 minutes. Remove the pan from the heat and set aside. **4. Whisk** the eggs and cream in a medium bowl. Season with salt and pepper and sprinkle with the cheese. **5. Drain** the pasta and add to the pan with the bacon. Return to high heat, add the egg mixture, and toss the briefly so that the eggs cook lightly but are still creamy. **6. Season** generously with pepper, sprinkle with extra cheese, and serve hot.

This is a classic Roman dish. There are many theories as to its origins, although most food historians think that it first appeared in Rome at the end of World War II when Allied troops brought a plentiful supply of fresh eggs and bacon to the famished city and local cooks adapted these ingredients to what they had on hand.

• **If you liked this recipe, try the tagliolini with mascarpone & eggs on page 82.**

PASTA

1 pound (500 g) bucatini

SAUCE

2 tablespoons extra-virgin olive oil · 8 ounces (250 g) pancetta, cut into thin strips · 1 onion, finely chopped · 2 pounds (1 kg) ripe tomatoes, peeled and chopped · 1–2 small dried chiles, crumbled · Salt and freshly ground white pepper

SERVES 4–6 · **PREPARATION** 20 MINUTES · **COOKING** 30–40 MINUTES

bucatini
all'amatriciana

SAUCE **1. Heat** the oil in a large frying pan over medium heat. Add the pancetta and sauté until pale golden brown, about 5 minutes. **2. Add** the onion and sauté until softened, 3–4 minutes. Add the tomatoes and chiles. Mix well and season with salt and pepper. **3. Cover** the pan and simmer over low heat until the tomatoes are reduced, about 30 minutes.

PASTA **4. Place** a large pot of salted water over high heat and bring to a boil. Cook the pasta in the boiling water until al dente, 10–12 minutes. **5. Drain** well and add to the sauce in the pan. Toss over high heat for 1 minute. **6. Serve** hot.

*This is another classic sauce.
It comes from the beautiful hilltown of
Amatrice in the rolling hills of Lazio.*

try the spaghetti alla puttanesca on page 24.

PASTA

1 pound (500 g) fusili

SAUCE

1 tablespoon butter • 12 ounces (350 g) Gorgonzola cheese, cut up
2/3 cup (150 ml) heavy (double) cream • Salt and freshly ground white pepper
1 cup (150 g) frozen peas • 1/2 cup (60 g) freshly grated Parmesan cheese

SERVES 4-6 • **PREPARATION** 15 MINUTES • **COOKING** 15-20 MINUTES

fusilli with
gorgonzola & peas

PASTA **1. Place** a large pot of salted water over high heat and bring to a boil.
SAUCE **2. Heat** the butter and Gorgonzola with the cream in a double boiler over barely simmering water until the cheese has melted. Season lightly with salt and a generous grinding of pepper. **3. Cook** the peas in a small pan of lightly salted water until tender, about 5 minutes. Drain well. **4. Cook** the pasta in the pot of boiling water until al dente, 10-12 minutes. **5. Drain** well and place in a heated serving bowl. Add the peas and cheese mixture and toss gently. **6. Sprinkle** with the Parmesan and serve hot.

Fusilli are ideal for this recipe because the creamy sauce and peas get caught in the spirals. You could also use conchiglie (shells), farfalle (bow ties), or ruote (wagon wheels).

try the conchiglie salad with blue cheese & apples on page 40.

PASTA

1 pound (500 g) spaghetti

SAUCE

**^{1}/$_2$ cup (120 ml) extra-virgin olive oil · 3 cloves garlic, finely chopped
6–8 anchovy fillets · 1 fresh red chile, seeded and finely chopped · 1 tablespoon
finely chopped fresh parsley · 2 pounds (1 kg) tomatoes, peeled and chopped
2 tablespoons tomato paste (concentrate) · 2 cups (200 g) black olives · 1 tablespoon brine-
cured capers · Freshly grated pecorino cheese**

SERVES 4–6 · **PREPARATION** 15 MINUTES · **COOKING** 20–25 MINUTES

spaghetti
alla puttanesca

PASTA **1. Place** a large pot of salted water over high heat and bring to a boil.

SAUCE **2. Heat** the oil in a large frying pan over medium heat. Add the garlic, anchovies, chile, and parsley and sauté until the anchovies have dissolved into the oil and garlic is pale gold, 2–3 minutes. **3. Add** the tomatoes, tomato paste, olives, and capers and simmer over low heat, stirring often, until reduced, 15–20 minutes. **4. Cook** the pasta in the pot of boiling water until al dente, 10–12 minutes. **5. Drain** well and transfer to the pan with the sauce. Toss over high heat for 1–2 minutes. **6. Serve** hot, sprinkled with the cheese.

This is a classic sauce in Naples and Rome. There are many theories about the origin of its picturesque name (literally "whore's sauce"), one of the most intriguing being that it was habitually served to clients at a famous bordello in the Quartieri Spagnoli, in Naples.

...cipe, try the cavatappi with spicy tomato sauce on page 42.

fusilli with sun-dried tomato & ricotta pesto

SERVES 4–6 · **PREPARATION** 15 MINUTES · **COOKING** 10–12 MINUTES

PASTA

1 pound (500 g) fusilli

RICOTTA PESTO

2 cups (500 g) fresh ricotta cheese, drained · 1 tablespoon finely chopped fresh mint · 1 tablespoon chopped fresh parsley · Salt and freshly ground black pepper · 4 ounces (120 g) sun-dried tomatoes, soaked in warm water for 10 minutes, drained, and chopped · 1–2 cloves garlic, finely chopped · 1 tablespoon salt-cured capers, rinsed · 1/3 cup (90 ml) extra-virgin olive oil · 3 cups (150 g) arugula (rocket), chopped + extra leaves, to garnish

PASTA **1. Place** a large pot of salted water over high heat and bring to a boil. Cook the pasta in the boiling water until al dente, 10–12 minutes.

RICOTTA PESTO **2. Combine** the ricotta, mint, and parsley in a small bowl and beat with a fork to make a smooth cream. Season with salt and pepper. **3. Combine** the sun-dried tomatoes in a small bowl with the garlic, capers, and oil, and mix well. **4. Combine** the arugula and tomato mixture in a food processor and chop until smooth. **5. Drain** the pasta and transfer to a heated serving bowl. **6. Add** the ricotta pesto and tomato mixture to the pasta and toss well. **7. Garnish** with the extra arugula and serve hot.

26

• If you liked this recipe, try the spaghetti with mediterranean pesto on page 46.

linguine with pesto, beans & potatoes

PASTA
1 pound (500 g) linguine

PESTO
2 tablespoons pine nuts · 1 cup (50 g) fresh basil leaves
1 clove garlic · 4 tablespoons freshly grated Parmesan cheese
1/2 cup (120 ml) extra-virgin olive oil · Salt and freshly ground black pepper

POTATOES & BEANS
14 ounces (400 g) green beans, chopped · 8 new potatoes, cut into 1/2-inch (1-cm) cubes
Freshly ground black pepper · 1/4 cup (30 g) shaved Parmesan cheese · Fresh basil leaves, to garnish

SERVES 4–6 · PREPARATION 20 MINUTES · COOKING 15–20 MINUTES

PASTA **1. Place** a large pot of salted water over high heat and bring to a boil. PESTO **2. Put** the pine nuts in a small frying pan and dry-fry until pale golden brown, 3–4 minutes. **3. Combine** the basil, garlic, Parmesan, and pine nuts in a food processor and chop until smooth. Gradually add the oil, beating until smooth. Season with salt and pepper.

POTATOES & BEANS **4. Cook** the green beans in a large pot of salted boiling water until just tender, 4–6 minutes. Drain well. **5. Cook** the pasta in the pot of boiling water for 5 minutes. Add the potatoes and cook until the pasta is al dente and the potatoes are tender, 5–7 minutes more. **6. Drain** and transfer to a large serving bowl with the beans and pesto. **7. Toss** well. Season with pepper, garnish with the Parmesan and basil, and serve hot.

This dish comes from Genoa, in northwestern Italy, the hometown of basil pesto. You can serve the linguine (or spaghetti) with just the pesto; the addition or potatoes and green beans is a traditional variation and makes a heartier meal.

• If you liked this recipe, try the linguine with walnut pesto on page 32.

farfalle salad with cherry tomatoes & feta

PASTA

1 pound (500 g) farfalle

SALAD

2 tablespoons extra-virgin olive oil · 20 cherry tomatoes, halved
1 tablespoon brine-cured capers · 8 ounces (250 g) feta cheese, cut into small
cubes · 1 cup (100 g) mixed black and green olives · 2 tablespoons finely chopped fresh
basil · 1 tablespoon finely chopped fresh mint · 2 cloves garlic, finely chopped
Small bunch scallions (spring onions), sliced

SERVES 4–6 · **PREPARATION** 15 MINUTES · **COOKING** 10–12 MINUTES

PASTA **1. Place** a large pot of salted water over high heat and bring to a boil. Cook the pasta in the boiling water until al dente, 10–12 minutes. SALAD **2. Combine** the oil, cherry tomatoes, capers, feta, olives, basil, mint, garlic, and scallions in a medium bowl. **3. Drain** the pasta and transfer to a large salad bowl. **4. Add** the tomato mixture, toss gently, and serve.

This makes a lovely, slightly warm salad. The feta cheese is heated through by the hot pasta and the flavors meld together beautifully.

• If you liked this recipe, try the conchiglie salad with blue cheese & apples on page 40.

linguine with **walnut pesto**

PASTA
1 pound (500 g) linguine

PESTO
1 cup (50 g) fresh basil leaves + extra whole leaves, to garnish
2 cloves garlic, chopped • 15 walnuts, shelled + extra walnut halves, to garnish
3 tablespoons pine nuts • ½ cup (120 ml) extra-virgin olive oil • ½ cup (60 g)
grated pecorino cheese + extra, to garnish • Freshly ground black pepper

SERVES 4–6 • **PREPARATION** 15 MINUTES • **COOKING** 10–12 MINUTES

PASTA **1. Place** a large pot of salted water over high heat and bring to a boil. Cook the pasta in the boiling water until al dente, 10–12 minutes. PESTO **2. Combine** the basil, garlic, walnuts, and pine nuts in a food processor and process until coarsely chopped. Gradually add the oil, processing until smooth. **3. Stir** in the cheese and season with pepper. **4. Drain** the pasta and transfer to a large heated serving bowl. **5. Add** the pesto and toss well. **6. Serve** hot, garnished with the basil, walnut halves, and extra cheese.

This walnut pesto is richer and nuttier than traditional basil pesto (see page 28).

• If you liked this recipe, try the linguine with pesto, beans & potatoes on page 28.

whole-wheat fusilli with veggies, feta & herbs

PASTA · 1 pound (500 g) whole-wheat (wholemeal) fusilli

SALAD · 8 tablespoons (120 ml) extra-virgin olive oil · 2 red bell peppers (capsicums), seeded and cut in small squares · 1 yellow bell pepper (capsicum), seeded and cut in small squares · 2 zucchini (courgettes), cut in small cubes · 5 ounces (150 g) feta cheese, cut in small cubes · 2-3 tablespoons finely chopped fresh mixed herbs (parsley, basil, mint, thyme) · 1 cup (100 g) black olives · Freshly ground black pepper

SERVES 4–6 · **PREPARATION** 15 MINUTES · **COOKING** 10–12 MINUTES

PASTA 1. **Place** a large pot of salted water over high heat and bring to a boil. **SALAD** 2. **Heat** 3 tablespoons of oil in a large frying pan over medium-high heat and sauté the bell peppers and zucchini until just tender, about 5 minutes. 3. **Cook** the pasta in the boiling water until al dente, 10–12 minutes. 4. **Drain** well and transfer to a large salad bowl. 5. **Add** the bell peppers, zucchini, cheese, herbs, and olives and toss well. 6. **Season** with pepper and serve warm.

Whole-wheat fusilli have more dietary fiber than ordinary fusilli and are better for your health. They are especially good in salads but most of the sauces in this book will also go beautifully with the nuttier flavors of whole-wheat pasta.

● If you liked this recipe, try the farfalle salad with cherry tomatoes & feta on page 30.

penne with
grilled summer veggies

PASTA

1 pound (500 g) penne rigate

SAUCE

2–3 red bell peppers (capsicums), seeded, cored, and quartered
1 large eggplant (aubergine), with skin, thinly sliced lengthwise • 2–3 zucchini
(courgettes) thinly sliced lengthwise • 1/3 cup (90 ml) extra-virgin olive oil
2–3 tablespoons finely chopped fresh basil • 1 tablespoon finely chopped fresh mint
+ extra leaves, to garnish • 1 clove garlic, finely chopped • Salt and freshly ground black pepper

SERVES 4–6 • **PREPARATION** 30 MINUTES • **COOKING** 25–30 MINUTES

PASTA **1. Place** a large pot of salted water over high heat and bring to a boil. SAUCE **2. Preheat** an overhead broiler (grill) and broil the bell peppers, turning them often, until the skins are blackened. Seal in a plastic food bag or wrap in aluminum foil for 10 minutes. Take out of the bag or foil and peel off the skins. **3. Heat** a grill pan (griddle) over medium-high heat. Brush the eggplant and zucchini lightly with half the oil and grill in batches until tender and marked with black lines, about 5 minutes each batch. **4. Cook** the pasta in the boiling water until al dente, 10–12 minutes. **5. Drain** well and transfer to a large serving bowl. **6. Chop** all the cooked vegetables coarsely. Add to the serving bowl with the pasta and toss gently. **7. Add** the basil, mint, and garlic. Season with salt and pepper and drizzle with the remaining oil. **8. Toss** well, garnish with the extra mint leaves, and serve hot.

This is a very tasty sauce for the summer months. It does take some time to prepare, but is well worth the effort. During the winter months, or if you are pressed for time, you could use well-drained bottled veggies.

● **If you liked this recipe, try the whole-wheat fusilli with veggies, feta & herbs on page 34.**

bucatini with leek & tomato sauce

PASTA

1 pound (500 g) bucatini

SAUCE

1/4 cup (60 ml) extra-virgin olive oil · 2 cloves garlic, finely chopped
3 large leeks, white parts only, thinly sliced · 2 pounds (1 kg) tomatoes, peeled
and chopped · Salt and freshly ground black pepper · 1 cup (120 g) coarsely grated
Scamorza (or other smoked) cheese · Fresh arugula (rocket) leaves, to garnish

SERVES 4–6 · **PREPARATION** 20 MINUTES · **COOKING** 30–40 MINUTES

SAUCE **1. Heat** the oil in a large frying pan over medium heat. Add the garlic and leeks and sauté until pale golden brown, about 5 minutes. **2. Add** the tomatoes and season with salt and pepper. Simmer over low heat until reduced, 25–30 minutes.

PASTA **3. Place** a large pot of salted water over high heat and bring to a boil. Cook the pasta in the boiling water until al dente, 10–12 minutes. **4. Drain** well and add to the pan with half the cheese. Toss over high heat for 1–2 minutes. **5. Garnish** with the arugula and remaining cheese and serve hot.

The leeks add a deliciously sweet flavor to this tomato sauce. If you like a spicy flourish, this sauce will absorb 1–2 crumbled dried chiles beautifully. Add them early on in the cooking time for a mellow bite, and toward the end for more punch.

38

● If you liked this recipe, try the bucatini all'amatriciana on page 20.

conchiglie salad with blue cheese & apples

PASTA

1 pound (500 g) conchiglie

SALAD

4–6 tender stalks celery, sliced · 8 ounces (250 g) blue cheese, cut in small cubes · 2 organic Granny Smith apples, cored and cut in small cubes · 1 cup (100 g) black olives · 4 tablespoons finely chopped fresh parsley · 2 cloves garlic, finely chopped · 1 tablespoon brine-cured green peppercorns (optional) · 1 tablespoon brine-cured capers · 2–3 tablespoons extra-virgin olive oil

SERVES 4–6 · PREPARATION 20 MINUTES + 5–10 MINUTES TO COOL · COOKING 10–12 MINUTES

PASTA **1. Place** a large pot of salted water over high heat and bring to a boil. Cook the pasta in the boiling water until al dente, 10–12 minutes.

SALAD **2. Combine** the celery, blue cheese, apples, olives, parsley, garlic, green peppercorns, if using, and capers in a medium bowl. **3. Drain** the pasta well and transfer to a large salad bowl. Add the oil and toss gently. Set aside to cool for 5–10 minutes. **4. Add** the celery mixture. Toss gently and serve.

Choose a ripe, tasty blue cheese, such as Danish, Gorgonzola piccante, or Roquefort for best results with this salad. If you are not using organic apples, either wash them very thoroughly or peel before cutting in cubes.

• If you liked this recipe, try the whole-wheat penne with pears & gorgonzola on page 50.

40

1 pound (500 g) cavatappi

SAUCE

1/3 cup (90 ml) extra-virgin olive oil · 5 ounces (150 g) pancetta, cut into small strips · 1–2 fresh red chiles, seeded and finely chopped · 5 cloves garlic, finely chopped · 2 pounds (1 kg) tomatoes, peeled and coarsely chopped · Salt 1–2 tablespoons finely chopped fresh parsley · 1/2 cup (60 g) freshly grated pecorino cheese

SERVES 4–6 · **PREPARATION** 20 MINUTES · **COOKING** 25–30 MINUTES

cavatappi with
spicy tomato sauce

PASTA **1. Place** a large pot of salted water over high heat and bring to a boil. SAUCE **2. Heat** the oil in a large frying pan over medium heat. Add the pancetta and sauté until crisp and golden, about 5 minutes. Using a slotted spoon, transfer the pancetta to a plate. **3. Sauté** the chiles and garlic in the same pan until the garlic is pale gold, 3–4 minutes. **4. Stir in** the tomatoes and season with salt. Add the parsley and simmer on low heat until the sauce is reduced, 15–20 minutes. Add the pancetta and simmer. **5. Cook** the pasta in the pot of boiling water until al dente, 10–12 minutes. **6. Drain** well and add to the sauce. Toss well. **7. Sprinkle** with the pecorino and serve hot.

This is a classic tomato and pancetta sauce. If preferred, use 2 (14-ounce/400-g) cans of tomatoes instead of the fresh tomatoes. You can serve it with a wide variety of short and long pasta shapes.

...cipe, try the whole-wheat spaghetti with spicy anchovy sauce on page 54.

1 pound (500 g) rigatoni

SAUCE

¹/₄ cup (60 ml) extra-virgin olive oil · 1 clove garlic, finely chopped
24 cherry tomatoes, halved · 1 cup (100 g) black olives · 1 tablespoon salt-cured
capers, rinsed · Salt and freshly ground black pepper · 8 ounces (250 g) fresh, creamy
goat cheese · 2–3 tablespoons coarsely chopped fresh basil

SERVES 4–6 · **PREPARATION** 15 MINUTES · **COOKING** 10–12 MINUTES

rigatoni with
tomatoes & goat cheese

PASTA **1. Place** a large pot of salted water over high heat and bring to a boil. Cook the pasta in the boiling water until al dente, 10–12 minutes.
SAUCE **2. Heat** the oil in a large frying pan over medium heat. Add the garlic and sauté until pale golden brown, 2–3 minutes. **3. Add** the cherry tomatoes, olives, and capers. Season with salt and pepper. Stir over high heat until the tomatoes are warmed, but still intact, 2–3 minutes.
4. Drain the pasta thoroughly and add to the pan with the tomatoes. **5. Stir in** the goat cheese and basil until creamy and well mixed. **6. Serve** hot.

If you don't like goat cheese, or you can't find it, you could replace it in this recipe with mascarpone cheese.

...cipe, try the farfalle salad with cherry tomatoes & feta on page 30.

spaghetti with mediterranean pesto

SERVES 4–6 · PREPARATION 15 MINUTES · COOKING 10–12 MINUTES

PASTA

1 pound (500 g) spaghetti

SAUCE

4 large ripe tomatoes, peeled and chopped · 2/3 cup (60 g) blanched almonds · 1 tablespoon chopped fresh mint · 3 tablespoons chopped fresh parsley · 1 tablespoon chopped fresh basil · 2 cloves garlic · 1 small fresh red chile, seeded and chopped · 6 tablespoons (90 ml) extra-virgin olive oil · Salt and freshly ground black pepper · 20 cherry tomatoes, halved · About 20 pickled caperberries, to garnish

PASTA **1. Place** a large pot of salted water over high heat and bring to a boil. Cook the pasta in the boiling water until al dente, 10–12 minutes.

SAUCE **2. Combine** the large tomatoes, almonds, mint, parsley, basil, 1 clove of garlic, chile, and 3 tablespoons of the oil in a food processor and chop until smooth. Season with salt and pepper. **3. Slice** the remaining clove of garlic. **4. Heat** the remaining oil in a large frying pan over medium heat and sauté the garlic and cherry tomatoes until the tomatoes have just softened, 2–3 minutes. **5. Drain** the pasta and add to the tomato mixture in the pan. Add the pesto and toss well. **6. Top** with the caperberries and serve hot.

Caperberries are the mature fruit of the Mediterranean caper bush. They are slightly less common than capers, which are made by pickling or salting the immature buds of the same fruit. Caperberries can be found in some supermarkets and gourmet food stores, and from online suppliers. Replace with capers if you can't find them.

● **If you liked this recipe, try the linguine with walnut pesto on page 32.**

46

rigatoni with tomatoes, ricotta & pesto

PASTA

¼ cup (60 ml) extra-virgin olive oil · 4 cloves garlic, finely chopped
24 cherry tomatoes, halved · 12 ounces (350 g) fresh ricotta cheese, at room
temperature, drained · ½ cup (120 ml) pesto (see page 28) · Salt and freshly ground
black pepper · Fresh basil leaves, to garnish

1 pound (500 g) rigatoni

SAUCE

SERVES 4–6 · **PREPARATION** 15 MINUTES · **COOKING** 10–12 MINUTES

PASTA **1. Place** a large pot of salted water over high heat and bring to a boil. Cook the pasta in the boiling water until al dente, 10–12 minutes.

SAUCE **2. Heat** the oil in a large frying pan over medium heat. Add the garlic and sauté until just beginning to color, 2–3 minutes. **3. Add** the cherry tomatoes and simmer over low heat until just softened but still intact, 3–4 minutes. **4. Drain** the pasta and place in a heated serving dish. **5. Add** the ricotta cheese, pesto, and cherry tomato mixture, and season with salt and pepper. **6. Toss** gently, garnish with the basil, and serve hot.

Technically, ricotta is not a cheese because it is made with the whey leftover from the cheese-making process. Use a very fresh ricotta made from skimmed milk in this recipe.

• If you liked this recipe, try rigatoni with tomatoes & goat cheese on page 44.

whole-wheat penne with
pears & gorgonzola

PASTA

1 pound (500 g) whole-wheat (wholemeal) penne

SAUCE

1/4 cup (60 g) butter • 8 ounces (250 g) Gorgonzola cheese, cut into 1/3 cup (90 ml) heavy (double) cream • 2 ripe organic pears, unpeeled and cut into small cubes • Freshly ground black pepper

SERVES 4–6 • **PREPARATION** 15 MINUTES • **COOKING** 10–12 MINUTES

PASTA **1. Place** a large pot of salted water over high heat and bring to a boil. Cook the pasta in the boiling water until al dente, 10–12 minutes. SAUCE **2. Melt** the butter in a medium saucepan over low heat. Add the Gorgonzola and cream and stir gently with a wooden spoon until the cheese is melted and creamy. heat. **3. Add** the pears, mix well, and remove from the bowl. Add the sauce and toss well. **4. Drain** the pasta and transfer to a large serving with black pepper and serve hot. **5. Season** generously

The nutty flavors of the whole-wheat pasta contrast delightfully with the sweet flesh of the pears and the creamy bite of the Gorgonzola.

• If you liked this recipe, try the conchiglie salad with blue cheese & apples on page 40.

50

whole-wheat spaghetti with pancetta & bell peppers

SERVES 4–6 · **PREPARATION** 25 MINUTES · **COOKING** 30–35 MINUTES

PASTA

1 pound (500 g) whole-wheat (wholemeal) spaghetti

SAUCE

1/3 cup (90 ml) extra-virgin olive oil · 3 ounces (90 g) pancetta, chopped
1 onion, finely chopped · 2 tablespoons finely chopped fresh parsley · 1 tablespoon chopped fresh basil + extra leaves, to garnish · 2 red bell peppers (capsicums), seeded and thinly sliced · 2 yellow bell peppers (capsicums), seeded and thinly sliced · 2 pounds (1 kg) tomatoes, peeled and chopped · 1 fresh red chile, thinly sliced · 1/2 teaspoon dried oregano
Salt · 1 cup (100 g) green olives, pitted and chopped · 1/2 cup (60 g) freshly grated Parmesan cheese

PASTA **1. Place** a large pot of salted water over high heat and bring to a boil.

SAUCE **2. Heat** the oil in a large frying pan over medium heat. Add the pancetta and sauté until lightly browned, 3–5 minutes. **3. Add** the onion, parsley, basil, and all the bell peppers. Sauté until the bell peppers and onion are softened, about 10 minutes. **4. Stir in** the tomatoes, chile, and oregano. Season with salt. Mix well, and simmer over medium heat until the tomatoes have broken down, 15–20 minutes. Add the olives. **5. Cook** the pasta in the pot of boiling water until al dente, 10–12 minutes. **6. Drain** well and add to the pan. Toss over high heat for 1 minute. **7. Sprinkle** with the cheese, garnish with the extra basil, and serve hot.

This versatile sauce will go equally well with plain spaghetti and with many other short and long pasta shapes too.

52

● If you liked this recipe, try the bucatini all'amatriciana on page 20.

whole-wheat spaghetti with spicy anchovy sauce

PASTA
1 pound (500 g) whole-wheat (wholemeal) spaghetti

SAUCE
1/3 cup (90 g) extra-virgin olive oil · 2 cloves garlic, finely chopped · 1–2 fresh red chiles, seeded and thinly sliced · 6–8 anchovy fillets · 2 pounds (1 kg) tomatoes, peeled and chopped · 1 cup (100 g) black olives · 2 tablespoons salt-cured capers, rinsed 1 tablespoon tomato paste (concentrate)

SERVES 4–6 · **PREPARATION** 15 MINUTES · **COOKING** 20–25 MINUTES

PASTA **1. Place** a large pot of salted water over high heat and bring to a boil. SAUCE **2. Heat** the oil in a large frying pan over medium heat. Add the garlic and chiles and sauté until the garlic is just beginning to color, 2–3 minutes. **3. Add** the anchovies and stir until dissolved in the oil. **4. Add** the tomatoes, olives, capers, and tomato paste. Simmer over low heat for 15 minutes. **5. Cook** the pasta in the pot of boiling water until al dente, 10–12 minutes. **6. Drain** the past well and add to the pan with the sauce. Toss over high heat for 1–2 minutes. **7. Serve** hot.

You won't need to season the sauce with salt; the anchovies, olives, and capers are all salty enough.

• **If you liked this recipe,** try spaghetti with mediterranean pesto on page 46.

54

PASTA

1 pound (500 g) spaghetti

SAUCE

$^1/_3$ cup (90 ml) extra-virgin olive oil • 1–2 small dried chiles, crumbled
5 ounces (150 g) pancetta, coarsely chopped • 1 large onion, finely chopped
1 cup (50 g) finely chopped fresh parsley • 1 cup (120 g) freshly grated pecorino cheese

SERVES 4–6 • **PREPARATION** 15 MINUTES • **COOKING** 10–12 MINUTES

spicy spaghetti with
pancetta & onion

PASTA **1. Place** a large pot of salted water over high heat and bring to a boil. Cook the pasta in the boiling water until al dente, 10–12 minutes.

SAUCE **2. Heat** the oil in a large frying pan over high heat. Sauté the chiles and pancetta until lightly browned, 3–4 minutes. Scoop out the pancetta with slotted spoon and set aside.

3. Sauté the onion in the same pan over medium heat until just softened, 3–4 minutes. **4. Return** the pancetta to the pan and simmer gently. **5. Drain** the pasta well and add to the pan. **6. Add** the parsley and half the pecorino and toss well. **7. Serve** hot, sprinkled with the remaining cheese.

Pancetta is the Italian answer to bacon. It is usually salt-cured and sometimes flavored with spices, such as cloves, peppercorns, or nutmeg. It is not normally smoked, although smoked versions do exist.

● If you liked this recipe, try the bucatini alla carbonara on page 18.

farfalle with tuna & olives

SERVES 4–6 • **PREPARATION** 25 MINUTES + 1 HOUR TO REST • **COOKING** 10–12 MINUTES

PASTA

1 pound (500 g) farfalle

SAUCE

24 cherry tomatoes, halved • Salt • 8 ounces (250 g) canned tuna, drained • 1 cup (100 g) mixed black and green olives • 2 scallions (spring onions), coarsely chopped • 1 stalk celery, sliced • 1 carrot, coarsely chopped • 1 clove garlic, finely chopped • 2 tablespoons finely chopped fresh parsley • 2 tablespoons coarsely chopped fresh basil + extra leaves, to garnish • Freshly ground black pepper • 1 teaspoon dried oregano • 1/4 cup (60 ml) extra-virgin olive oil

SAUCE 1. **Sprinkle** the tomatoes with salt. Put in a colander and let rest for 1 hour. PASTA 2. **Place** a large pot of salted water over high heat and bring to a boil. 3. **Put** the tuna in a medium bowl and crumble with a fork. Add the cherry tomatoes, olives, scallions, celery, carrot, garlic, parsley, and basil. Season with salt, pepper, and oregano. 4. **Cook** the pasta in the boiling water until al dente, 10–12 minutes. 5. **Drain** well and let cool in the colander for 5 minutes. 6. **Transfer** the pasta to a large salad bowl. Add the tuna mixture, drizzle with the oil, and toss well. 7. **Garnish** with extra basil and serve.

You can also prepare this salad several hours ahead of time and chill in the refrigerator until about 30 minutes before serving,

• If you liked this recipe, try the rigatoni with tomatoes & goat cheese on page 44.

spaghetti with **squid ink**

SERVES 4–6 · **PREPARATION** 30 MINUTES · **COOKING** 1¾ HOURS

PASTA

1 pound (500 g) spaghetti

SAUCE

1 pound (500 g) squid or cuttlefish · ¼ cup (60 ml) extra-virgin olive oil
2 cloves garlic, finely chopped · 3 tablespoons finely chopped fresh parsley
1-2 dried red chiles, crumbled · ⅓ cup (90 ml) white wine · 1 tablespoon tomato paste
(concentrate) · Salt · ⅓ cup (90 ml) hot water

SAUCE **1. To clean the squid**, reach inside the bodies and pull everything out, taking care not to damage the small silver-gray sac—the ink bladder—located near the top of the body. Be sure to remove the transparent quill inside. **2. Cut off the** tentacles just below the eyes. Reserve the tentacles and the ink sac and discard the rest of the innards. **3. Cut** the bodies and tentacles into small pieces. **4. Heat** the oil in a medium saucepan over medium heat. Add the garlic and sauté until pale gold, about 3 minutes. **5. Add** the squid, tablespoons of parsley, and chiles. Cover and simmer over low

heat for 45 minutes. **6. Pour** half the wine into a small bowl, add the tomato paste, and stir until it dissolves. Add to the saucepan. **7. Simmer** for 20 minutes. Season with salt and add the hot water. Cover and simmer for 30 more minutes. **8. Remove** the ink from the squid sacs, mix with the remaining wine, and add it to the sauce. PASTA **9. Place** a large pot of salted water over high heat and bring to a boil. Cook the pasta in the boiling water until al dente, 10–12 minutes. **10. Drain** well and add to the pan with the sauce, mixing well. **11. Serve** hot, garnished with the remaining parsley.

• If you liked this recipe, try the spaghetti with seafood al cartoccio on page 72.

linguine with tomatoes & clams

PASTA
1 pound (500 g) linguine

SAUCE
2 pounds (1 kg) clams, in shell, soaked in cold water for 1 hour
1/3 cup (90 ml) extra-virgin olive oil · 4 cloves garlic, finely chopped · 1 fresh red chile, seeded and thinly sliced · 6 large tomatoes, sliced · 1/3 cup (90 ml) dry white wine
· Salt · 3 tablespoons finely chopped fresh parsley

SERVES 4–6 · **PREPARATION** 15 MINUTES + 1 HOUR TO SOAK · **COOKING** 25–30 MINUTES

PASTA **1. Place** a large pot of salted water over high heat and bring to a boil.
SAUCE **2. Place** the clams in a large pan over medium heat with a little water. Cook until they open, 5–10 minutes. Discard any clams that do not open. Remove from the heat and discard most of the clam shells. Leave a few mollusks in their shells to garnish. **3. Heat** the oil in a large frying pan over medium heat. Add the garlic and chile and sauté until pale golden brown, 3–4 minutes. **4. Add** the tomatoes and wine, season with salt, and simmer until the tomatoes begin to break down, about 15 minutes. **5. Place** the clams in the pan and stir well. **6. Cook** the pasta in the pot of boiling water until al dente, 10–12 minutes. **7. Drain** and add to the pan with the sauce. Toss over high heat for 1–2 minutes. **8. Serve** hot.

Unless the clams have already been cleaned, you will need to soak them in cold water for about an hour to remove the sand and mud they often contain.

• If you liked this recipe, try the spaghetti with clams & arugula on page 64.

62

spaghetti with clams & arugula

PASTA

1 pound (500 g) spaghetti

SAUCE

2 tablespoons extra-virgin olive oil · 2 cloves garlic, finely chopped · 1/3 cup (90 ml) dry white wine · 1-2 fresh red chiles, seeded and finely chopped · Salt

2 pounds (1 kg) clams, in shell, soaked in cold water for 1 hour · 2 cups (100 g) arugula (rocket) · Parmesan shavings, to serve · Freshly ground black pepper

SERVES 4–6 · PREPARATION 25 MINUTES + 1 HOUR TO SOAK · COOKING 10–12 MINUTES

PASTA 1. Place a large pot of salted water over high heat and bring to a boil. Cook the pasta in the boiling water until al dente, 10–12 minutes. SAUCE **2. Heat** the oil in a large frying pan over medium-high heat. Add the clams, garlic, and wine, cover, and cook until the clams are all open, about 5 minutes. Shake the pan from time to

time. Discard any clams that do not open. **3. Add** the chiles and remove the clams from most of the shells, leaving a few in their shells to make the finished dish look more attractive. Leave a few of the clams. Add the arugula and the pasta and add to the pan with the clams. **4. Drain** toss until wilted slightly. **5. Serve** hot, topped with the Parmesan and plenty of black pepper.

If liked, add about 12 cherry tomatoes (halved) to the sauce with the arugula.

• If you liked this recipe, try the linguine with mussels on page 70.

ruote with
shrimp & zucchini

PASTA
1 pound (500 g) ruote

SAUCE
1/4 cup (60 ml) extra-virgin olive oil · 1 small onion, finely chopped
3 medium zucchini (courgettes), thinly sliced · Salt and freshly ground black
pepper · 12 ounces (350 g) shrimp (prawns), shelled, deveined, and cooked
1/2 cup (120 ml) light (single) cream · 2 tablespoons finely chopped fresh parsley

SERVES 4–6 · **PREPARATION** 15 MINUTES · **COOKING** 12–15 MINUTES

PASTA **1. Place** a large pot of salted water over high heat and bring to a boil. Cook the pasta in the boiling water until al dente, 10–12 minutes.

SAUCE **2. Heat** the oil in a large frying pan over medium heat. Add the onion and sauté until softened, 3–4 minutes. **3. Add** the zucchini and season with salt and pepper. Simmer over medium-high heat until almost tender, 3–4 minutes, stirring often. **4. Add** the shrimp and simmer, stirring often, until heated through, 2–3 minutes. **5. Stir in** the cream and cook until heated through, about 1 minute. **6. Drain** the pasta and add to the pan with the sauce. Sprinkle with the parsley and toss well. **7. Serve** hot.

Ruote, also known as wagon wheels, are perfect in this dish, but you could also use farfalle, conchiglie, or cavatappi.

• **If you liked this recipe, try** the farfalle with tuna & olives on page 58.

PASTA

1 pound (500 g) spaghettini

SAUCE

**6 tablespoons (90 ml) extra-virgin olive oil · 3 cloves garlic, finely
chopped · 1 fresh red chile, seeded and finely chopped · 8 ounces (250 g) fresh
cooked crabmeat or canned crabmeat, drained · ½ cup (120 ml) dry white wine
Salt and freshly ground black pepper · 4 tablespoons finely chopped fresh parsley
Finely grated zest of 1 unwaxed lemon**

SERVES *4–6* **· PREPARATION** 15 MINUTES **· COOKING** 10 MINUTES

Spaghettini with
crab & lemon

PASTA **1. Place** a large pot of salted water over high heat and bring to a boil. Cook the pasta in the boiling water until al dente, 7–8 minutes. SAUCE **2. Heat** 3 tablespoons of oil in a large frying pan over medium heat. Add the garlic and chile and sauté until the garlic is pale gold, 3–4 minutes. **3. Add** the crabmeat and wine, season with salt and pepper, and sauté until heated through, 2–3 minutes. **4. Drain** the pasta, add to the pan with the crabmeat, and toss well. **5. Drizzle** with the remaining 3 tablespoons of oil, and sprinkle with the parsley and lemon zest. **6. Serve** hot.

Spaghettini are thinner than normal spaghetti and they go well with this delicate sauce. However, you could also use plain spaghetti or linguine.

68

• If you liked this recipe, try the ruote with shrimp & zucchini on page 66.

PASTA

1 pound (500 g) linguine

SAUCE

2 pounds (1 kg) mussels, in shell, soaked in cold water for 1 hour

1/3 cup (90 ml) dry white wine · 1/2 cup (120 ml) extra-virgin olive oil

4–6 cloves garlic, finely chopped · 5 tablespoons finely chopped fresh parsley

Salt and freshly ground black pepper

SERVES 4–6 · PREPARATION 25 MINUTES + 1 HOUR TO SOAK · COOKING 15 MINUTES

linguine with
mussels

PASTA **1. Place** a large pot of salted water over high heat and bring to a boil. SAUCE **2. Put** the mussels in a large saucepan, drizzle with the wine, cover, and cook over medium-high heat until they open up, 5–10 minutes. Discard any mussels that have not opened. **3. Strain** the mussel liquid through a fine-metal sieve and set aside. Remove the mussels from their shells and set aside in a bowl. **4. Heat** the oil in a large frying pan over medium heat. Add the garlic and 3 tablespoons of parsley and sauté until the garlic is just beginning to color.

Season with salt and pepper, and set asi... pot of boiling... until almost al dente, 8–10... **6. Drain** and add... with the... parsl... hi... th...

5. Cook the pasta in the pot of boiling...

garnished with...

70

spaghetti with seafood al cartoccio

PASTA

14 ounces (400 g) small squid, cleaned · 1/3 cup (90 ml) extra-virgin olive oil · 2 cloves garlic, finely chopped · 1 dried chile, crumbled · 2 tablespoons finely chopped fresh parsley · 1/2 cup (120 ml) dry white wine · 1 1/2 pounds (750 g) firm-ripe tomatoes, peeled and chopped · 1 1/2 pounds (750 g) clams, in shell, soaked in cold water for 1 hour · 1 1/2 pounds (750 g) mussels, in shell, soaked in cold water for 1 hour · Salt

PASTA

1 pound (500 g) spaghetti

SAUCE

SERVES 8 · PREPARATION 25 MINUTES + 1 HOUR TO SOAK · COOKING 30–40 MINUTES

PASTA **1. Place** a large pot of salted water over high heat and bring to a boil.

SAUCE **2. Preheat** the oven to 350°F (180°C/gas 4). **3. Remove** the mottled skin from the squid and cut the bodies into small chunks. Cut the tentacles in half. **4. Heat** the oil in a large saucepan over medium heat. Add the garlic, chile, and parsley and sauté until the garlic is pale gold, 2–3 minutes. **5. Pour in** the wine and let it evaporate. Add the tomatoes and simmer for 10 minutes. **6. Add** the squid, clams, and mussels. Season with salt. Cover and simmer over medium heat until the clams and mussels open up, 5–10 minutes. Remove from the heat and discard any clams or mussels that haven't opened. Extract half the shellfish from their shells. **7. Cook** the spaghetti in the boiling water for half the time indicated on the package. Drain the spaghetti, reserving the cooking water, and add to the seafood sauce. **8. Cut** 8 large pieces of aluminum foil or parchment paper and fold each one in half to double the thickness. **9. Divide** the pasta and seafood sauce into eight portions and place in the center of the pieces of foil or paper, adding 3 tablespoons of reserved cooking water to each portion. Close up, sealing well. There should be a small air pocket inside each of the packages. **10. Bake** for 12–15 minutes, until puffed up slightly. **11. Serve** the packages directly on the table for your guests to open.

"Al cartoccio" means "in parchment" and refers to a method of cooking food by wrapping it in parchment paper or aluminum foil and baking it. In English we often use the French term "en papillote" for the same technique.

• **If you liked this recipe, try the linguine with mussels on page 70.**

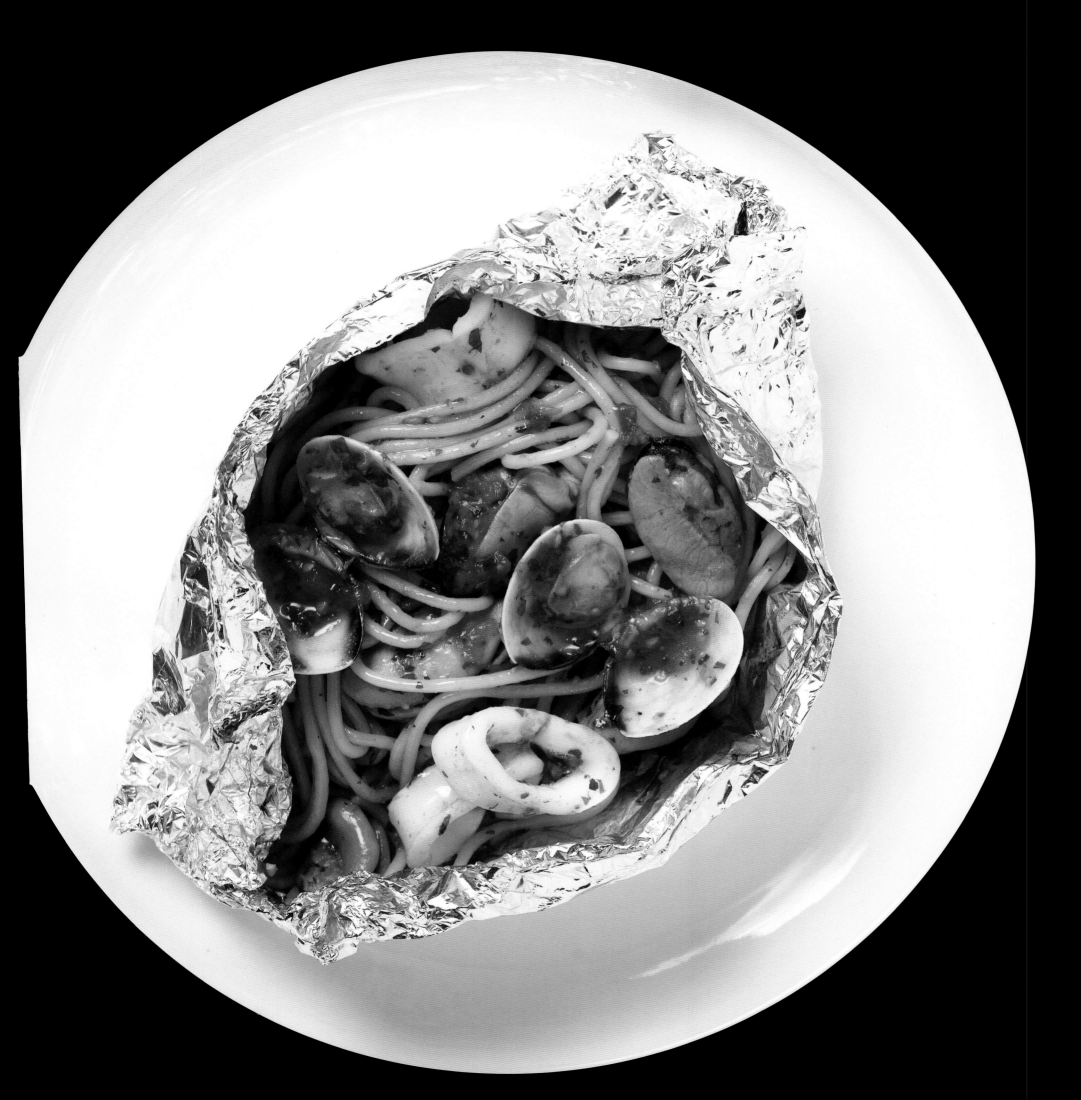

spaghetti with meatballs

SERVES 4–6 · **PREPARATION** 15 MINUTES · **COOKING** 3¼ HOURS

PASTA
1 pound (500 g) spaghetti

SAUCE
¼ cup (60 ml) extra-virgin olive oil · 1 small onion, finely
1 carrot, finely chopped · 2 tablespoons finely chopped fresh par
leaves, to garnish · 12 ounces (350 g) beef, in a single cut · 2 pounds (

MEATBALLS
tomatoes, peeled and chopped · Salt

12 ounces (350 g) ground (minced) beef · 1 large egg · 1 cup (120 g) freshly grated Parmesan
4 cups (250 g) fresh bread crumbs · ¼ teaspoon freshly grated nutmeg · 1 cup (250 ml) olive oil, to

SAUCE **1. Heat** the oil in a large
frying pan over medium heat. Add
the onion, carrot, and parsley and
sauté until softened, 3–4 minutes.
2. Add the beef and sauté until
browned all over, 8–10 minutes.
3. Add the tomatoes and season with
salt. Simmer over low heat until the
meat is very tender, about 3 hours.
Remove the meat. It can be served
separately, after the pasta.
MEATBALLS **4. Mix** the ground beef, egg,
Parmesan, bread crumbs, and nutmeg in a

large bowl until well blended. Shape
the mixture into balls about the
size of marbles. **5. Heat** the frying
oil in a large frying pan. Fry the
meatballs in small batches until
golden brown, 5–7 minutes each
batch. Drain on paper towels.
PASTA **6. Place** a large pot of salted
water over high heat and bring to a boil.
Cook the pasta until al dente, 10–12
minutes. **7. Drain** thoroughly and add to the pan
with the sauce. Add the meatballs and toss gently.
8. Serve hot, garnished with the parsley.

*This is a classic dish from southern Italy. It takes
some time to cook, but makes a truly special
meal. It Italy, the spaghetti and meatballs are
served as a first course and the meat from the
sauce is served as the main, usually with
vegetables or a salad.*

● **if you liked this recipe**, try the maltagliati with tomato & sausage sauce on page 100.

74

PASTA

1½ pounds (750 g) spaghetti

SAUCE

2 tablespoons extra-virgin olive oil · 2 large onions, finely chopped
2 cloves garlic, finely chopped · 1½ pounds (750 g) ground (minced) beef
1 tablespoon chili powder · 1 teaspoon ground allspice · 1 teaspoon ground cinnamon
1 teaspoon ground cumin · ½ teaspoon cayenne pepper · ½ teaspoon salt · 1½ tablespoons
unsweetened cocoa powder · 1 (14-ounce/400-g) can tomatoes, with juice · 1 tablespoon
Worcestershire sauce · 1 tablespoon cider vinegar · ½ cup (120 ml) water + extra, as required
1 (14-ounce/400-g) can red kidney beans, drained · 1 cup (120 g) freshly grated tasty cheese, to serve

SERVES 8 · PREPARATION 25 MINUTES · COOKING 2 HOURS

spaghetti with cincinnati chili

SAUCE **1. Heat** the oil in a large saucepan over medium heat. Add half the onion, garlic, beef, and chili powder and sauté until the beef is browned, 5–6 minutes. **2. Add the** allspice, cinnamon, cumin, cayenne, salt, cocoa, tomatoes, Worcestershire sauce, cider vinegar, and water. Reduce the heat to low and simmer for 2 hours. Stir often, and add a little extra water if the sauce dries out too much.

PASTA **3. Place** a large pot of salted water over high heat and bring to a boil. Cook the pasta in the boiling water until al dente, 10–12 minutes. **4. Heat** the beans in a small saucepan over medium heat until warmed through. **5. Drain** the pasta and divide evenly among eight serving dishes. Ladle the chili over the top. Top with beans and sprinkle with the cheese and remaining onion. **6. Serve** hot.

This regional US dish lies somewhere between Chili con carne and Spaghetti bolognese. Whatever its origins, it makes a splendid family meal and is perfect when you have a mob to feed.

● If you liked this recipe, try the spaghetti with meatballs on page 74.

PASTA

1 pound (500 g) cavatelli

SAUCE

**3 tablespoons extra-virgin olive oil · 1 onion, finely chopped · 2 cloves
garlic, finely chopped · 3¹/2 ounces (100 g) diced pancetta · 2 pounds (1 kg)
tomatoes, peeled and chopped, or 2 (14-ounce/400-g) cans tomatoes, with juice
1 cup (180 g) sun-dried tomatoes, coarsely chopped · 1 tablespoon coarsely chopped fresh basil
Salt and freshly ground black pepper · 1 bunch arugula (rocket)
Parmesan cheese, in shavings, to serve**

SERVES 4–6 · **PREPARATION** 15 MINUTES · **COOKING** 20–30 MINUTES

cavatelli with
pancetta & tomato sauce

78

PASTA **1. Place** a large pot of salted water over high heat and bring to a boil.
SAUCE **2. Heat** the oil in a large frying pan over medium heat. Add the onion, garlic, and pancetta and sauté until pale golden brown, about 5 minutes. **3. Add** the fresh or canned tomatoes, sun-dried tomatoes, and basil.

Season with salt and pepper and simmer over low heat until reduced, 15–20 minutes. **4. Cook** the pasta in the pot of boiling water until al dente, 8–10 minutes. **5. Drain** well and add to the pan with the tomato sauce. Add the arugula and toss until wilted 1–2 minutes. **6. Serve** hot, topped with the Parmesan.

*Cavatelli are a small, shell-shaped pasta from
Molise and Puglia in southern Italy. If you can't find
them, you can replace them in this recipe with
fusilli, rigatoni, or farfalle.*

● If you liked this recipe, try the cavatappi with spicy tomato sauce on page 42.

orecchiette with **broccoli**

PASTA
1 pound (500 g) orecchiette

SAUCE
1½ pounds (750 g) broccoli, cut into small florets · 4 tablespoons
(60 ml) extra-virgin olive oil · 6 scallions (spring onions), finely chopped
2 tablespoons pine nuts · 2 tablespoons finely chopped fresh parsley + extra leaves,
to garnish · 2 tablespoons currants · 1 cup (250 ml) dry white wine · 1 teaspoon saffron
dissolved in 1/2 cup (120 ml) water · Salt and freshly ground black pepper · 5 anchovy fillets,
crumbled · 2 ounces (60 g) Parmesan, in shavings

SERVES 4–6 · PREPARATION 15 MINUTES · COOKING 15-20 MINUTES

PASTA **1. Place** a large pot of salted water over high heat
and bring to a boil.
SAUCE **2. Blanch** the broccoli in the boiling water for 2
minutes. Scoop out with a slotted spoon and set aside.
Return the water to a boil. **3. Heat** 2 tablespoons of oil
in a large frying pan over medium heat. Add the scallions
and sauté until softened, 3-4 minutes. **4. Add** the pine
nuts, parsley, and currants and simmer for 2 minutes.
5. Pour in the wine and simmer until it evaporates.
Add the broccoli and saffron water. Season with salt
and pepper. Simmer for 10 minutes. **6. Cook** the
pasta in the pot of boiling water until al dente,
10-12 minutes. **7. Heat** the remaining 2
tablespoons of oil in a small saucepan over
medium heat. Add the anchovy mixture
and stir until dissolved in the oil.
8. Stir the anchovy mixture into
the broccoli sauce. **9. Drain** the pasta and add to the pan
with the sauce. Toss well. **10. Top** with the Parmesan
cheese, garnish with the parsley, and serve hot.

*Orecchiette ("little ears" in Italian) come from the
Puglia region, which is the heel on the boot of the
Italian peninsula. They are available
fresh or dried. Consult the
package for the correct
cooking time. Replace with
penne rigate or fusilli,
if preferred.*

• If you liked this recipe, try the linguine with walnut pesto on page 32.

80

tagliolini with mascarpone & eggs

SERVES 4 · **PREPARATION** 15 MINUTES + TIME TO MAKE THE PASTA · **COOKING** 7–8 MINUTES

PASTA

14 ounces (400 g) fresh tagliolini, storebought or homemade (see pages 6–7)

SAUCE

1 cup (250 g) mascarpone cheese · 3 very fresh large egg yolks

½ cup (60 g) freshly grated Parmesan cheese · Salt · ¼ teaspoon freshly grated nutmeg

Freshly ground black pepper, to serve · Sprigs of fresh parsley, to garnish

PASTA 1. Prepare the tagliolini following the instructions on pages 6–7, or use storebought pasta, as preferred. **2. Place** a large pot of salted water over high heat and bring to a boil. **SAUCE 3. Mix** the mascarpone and egg yolks in a large heatproof bowl. Place in a pan over barely simmering water and heat until the egg mixture registers 160°F (80°C) on an instant-read thermometer. Remove from the heat and let cool a little. **4. Add** the Parmesan and season with salt and nutmeg. **5. Cook** the tagliolini in the pot of boiling water until al dente, 2–3 minutes. **6. Drain** well and transfer to a heated serving dish. **7. Stir** the mascarpone mixture into the tagliolini, tossing gently. **8. Serve** hot, seasoned with plenty of black pepper and garnished with parsley.

This rich and creamy sauce also goes well with plain or spinach tagliatelle.

• **If you liked this recipe, try the bucatini alla carbonara on page 18.**

watercress tagliolini with pesto

PASTA

8 ounces (250 g) watercress + extra, to garnish · 1²/₃ cups (250 g) all-purpose (plain) flour · 1¹/₂ cups (250 g) whole-wheat (wholemeal) flour · ¹/₂ teaspoon salt
3/4 cup (180 ml) water

PESTO

1¹/₂ cups (75 g) fresh basil · ¹/₄ cup (60 ml) extra-virgin olive oil · 3 ounces (90 g) cream cheese
4 tablespoons pine nuts · 3 cloves garlic

SERVES 4–6 · PREPARATION 45 MINUTES + 1 HOUR TO REST · COOKING 4–6 MINUTES

PASTA **1. Cook** the watercress in a pan of lightly salted boiling water until tender, 2–3 minutes. Drain and finely chop in a food processor. **2. Combine** both flours with the salt in a large bowl. Add the watercress and stir in the water until a firm dough forms. **3. Transfer** to a floured work surface and knead until smooth and elastic, about 10 minutes. **4. Wrap** in plastic wrap (cling film) and let rest for 1 hour. **5. Divide** the dough into six pieces and roll each one through a pasta machine, reducing the thickness setting by one notch each time, until you reach the second thinnest setting. **6. Put** the pasta machine on the setting for tagliolini (thin ribbons) and cut each sheet. Fold into "nests"

7. Place a large pot of salted water over high heat and bring to a boil. PESTO **8. Combine** the basil, oil, cream cheese, pine nuts, and garlic in a food processor and process until smooth. **9. Cook** the tagliolini in the pot of boiling water until al dente, 2–3 minutes. **10. Drain** well and transfer to a heated serving bowl. Add the pesto and toss gently. **11. Serve** hot, garnished with extra watercress.

These watercress tagliolini are superb, but they take some time and skill to prepare. If you are rushed for time, use 14 ounces (400 g) of storebought plain or spinach tagliatelle and serve with the creamy pesto.

• If you liked this recipe, try the spinach gnocchi with tomato sauce on page 124.

spicy tagliatelle with eggplant sauce

PASTA

2²/3 cups (400 g) all-purpose (plain) flour · 4 very fresh large eggs · 2 dried chiles, crumbled
1 teaspoon finely chopped fresh thyme

SAUCE

3 medium eggplant (aubergines), peeled and cut into 1-inch (2.5-cm) cubes
1/3 cup (90 ml) extra-virgin olive oil · 2 cloves garlic, finely chopped · 1 sprig fresh thyme
3 tablespoons coarsely chopped fresh basil + extra leaves, to garnish · Salt and freshly ground white
pepper · 3 ripe tomatoes, peeled and chopped · 6 tablespoons freshly grated pecorino cheese

SERVES 4 · PREPARATION 45 MINUTES + 1 HOUR TO REST · COOKING 20-30 MINUTES

PASTA **1. Prepare** the tagliatelle following the instructions on pages 6-7, adding the chiles and thyme to the eggs. Let rest for at least 1 hour. **2. Place** a large pot of salted water over high heat and bring to a boil. SAUCE **3. Boil** the eggplant in lightly salted water for 4 minutes. Drain, squeezing out the excess moisture. **4. Heat** the oil in a large frying pan over medium heat. Add the garlic and thyme and sauté for 2 minutes. **5. Add** the eggplant and simmer for 6-7 minutes, mashing gently with the back of a fork. **6. Remove** from the heat, add the basil, and season with salt and pepper. Let cool a little and then chop in a food processor until smooth. **7. Return** the eggplant cream to the frying pan over medium heat and add the tomatoes. Simmer until the tomatoes have broken down and the sauce is creamy, 5-10 minutes. **8. Cook** the pasta in the boiling water until al dente, about 3-4 minutes. **9. Drain** well and add to the pan with the sauce. Sprinkle with the cheese and toss gently. **10.** Serve hot, garnished with the basil leaves.

You can serve the eggplant sauce with plain tagliatelle, if preferred. If you want a spicy sauce, add 1-2 crumbled dried chiles along with the tomatoes.

• If you liked this recipe, try the watercress tagliolini with pesto on page 84.

tagliatelle caprese

SERVES 4 · **PREPARATION** 15 MINUTES + TIME TO MAKE THE PASTA · **COOKING** 3–4 MINUTES

PASTA

14 ounces (400 g) fresh tagliatelle, storebought or homemade (see pages 6–7)

SAUCE

2 pounds (1 kg) tomatoes, diced · 4 tablespoons capers, rinsed · 7 ounces (200 g) fresh mozzarella cheese, drained and diced · 1 tablespoon balsamic or red wine vinegar · ¼ cup (60 ml) extra-virgin olive oil · 1 tablespoon salt-cured capers, coarsely chopped fresh basil · Salt and freshly ground black pepper

PASTA **1. Prepare** the tagliatelle following the instructions on pages 6–7, or use storebought pasta, as preferred. **2. Place** a large pot of salted water over high heat and bring to a boil.

SAUCE **3. Combine** the tomatoes, basil, mozzarella, capers, oil, and vinegar in a bowl. Season with salt and pepper. **4. Cook** the pasta in the pot of boiling water until al dente, 3–4 minutes. **5. Drain** well and place in a large bowl. Add the tomato mixture and toss gently. **6. Serve** hot.

This fresh, light sauce takes it name from the classic Italian salad—Insalata Caprese—itself named for the beautiful island of Capri off the coast of Naples. Be sure to use very good quality, fresh mozzarella cheese.

● If you liked this recipe, try the penne with tomatoes & mozzarella on page 16.

tagliatelle with
salmon, cream & peas

PASTA
14 ounces (400 g) fresh tagliatelle,
storebought or homemade (see pages 6–7)

SAUCE
1 cup (150 g) frozen peas · ¼ cup (60 ml) dry white wine · 1¼ cups (300 ml)
heavy (double) cream · 8 slices smoked salmon · 3 scallions (spring onions), finely
chopped · Freshly ground black pepper

SERVES 4 · **PREPARATION** 15 MINUTES + TIME TO MAKE THE PASTA · **COOKING** 5–10 MINUTES

PASTA **1. Prepare** the tagliatelle following the instructions on pages 6–7, or use storebought pasta, as preferred. **2. Place** a large pot of salted water over high heat and bring to a boil.

SAUCE **3. Blanch** the peas in a pot of boiling water for 2 minutes. Drain well and set aside. **4. Bring** the wine to a boil in a large frying pan. Stir in 1 cup (250 ml) of cream and simmer until the sauce reduces and thickens, 3–4 minutes. **5. Chop** four slices of smoked salmon with the scallions and remaining ¼ cup (60 ml) of cream in a food processor. **6. Stir** the salmon mixture into the sauce and simmer until heated through. **7. Cut** the remaining salmon slices into strips. Add to the sauce along with the peas. Season with pepper. **8. Cook** the pasta in the pot of boiling water until al dente, 3–4 minutes. **9. Drain** well and add to the pan with the sauce. Toss gently. **10. Serve** hot with plenty of freshly ground black pepper.

This quick and easy sauce is as elegant as it is delicious.

• If you liked this recipe, try the smoked salmon ravioli with lemon & dill sauce on page 104.

tagliatelle with scallops & bread crumbs

PASTA

14 ounces (400 g) fresh tagliatelle, storebought or homemade (see pages 6–7)

SAUCE

12 fresh sea scallops, preferably with their corals · 8 tablespoons (120 ml) extra-virgin olive oil · 1/2 cup (60 g) fine dry bread crumbs · 4 tablespoons finely chopped fresh parsley · 2 cloves garlic, finely chopped · 1 teaspoon red pepper flakes · 1/4 cup (60 ml) dry white wine

SERVES 4 · **PREPARATION** 15 MINUTES + TIME TO MAKE THE PASTA · **COOKING** 10–12 MINUTES

PASTA 1. Prepare the tagliatelle following the instructions on pages 6–7, or use storebought pasta, as preferred. **2. Place** a large pot of salted water over high heat and bring to a boil.

SAUCE 3. Detach the corals from the scallops and set aside. **4. Heat** 2 tablespoons of oil in a small frying pan over medium heat. Add the bread crumbs and fry until golden, about 3 minutes. Remove and set aside. **5. Heat** the remaining 6 tablespoons (90 ml) of oil in the same frying pan over medium heat. Add 2 tablespoons of parsley,

the garlic, and red pepper flakes and sauté for 2 minutes. **6. Cook** the pasta in the boiling water until al dente, 3–4 minutes. **7. Add** the white parts of the scallops to the sauce. Cook until they start to turn opaque, about 30 seconds. **8. Increase** the heat. Add the wine and the reserved scallop corals. Simmer for 30 seconds. **9. Drain** the pasta and add to the pan with the sauce. Toss gently. Sprinkle with the bread crumbs and remaining 2 tablespoons of parsley. **10. Serve** hot.

If you don't like spicy food, just leave the red pepper flakes out of this dish. The sweet flavor of the scallops goes beautifully with the crisp bread crumbs either way.

● *If you liked this recipe, try the spaghettini with crab & lemon on page 68.*

tagliatelle with bolognese meat sauce

PASTA

14 ounces (400 g) fresh tagliatelle, storebought or homemade (see pages 6–7)

BOLOGNESE MEAT SAUCE

3 tablespoons extra-virgin olive oil · 2 tablespoons butter · 4 ounces (120 g) diced pancetta · 1 small onion, finely chopped · 1 small carrot, finely chopped · 1 stalk celery, finely chopped · 1 clove garlic, finely chopped · 1 pound (500 g) ground (minced) beef ½ cup (120 ml) dry white wine · 2 tablespoons tomato paste (concentrate) · ½ cup (120 ml) beef stock · Salt and freshly ground black pepper · ½ cup (120 ml) milk · ¼ cup (30 g) freshly grated Parmesan

SERVES 4 · PREPARATION 45 MINUTES + TIME TO MAKE THE PASTA · COOKING 2–3 HOURS

PASTA 1. Prepare the tagliatelle following the instructions on pages 6–7, or use storebought pasta, as preferred.
BOLOGNESE MEAT SAUCE
2. Heat the oil and butter in a large saucepan over medium heat. Add the pancetta, onion, carrot, celery, and garlic and sauté until the vegetables have softened, about 5 minutes.
3. Add the beef and sauté until browned, about 5 minutes.
4. Pour in the wine and simmer until it evaporates, 2–3 minutes. Mix in the tomato paste and beef stock. Season with salt and pepper. Return to a boil. Simmer over very low heat for 2–3 hours, stirring occasionally. Add 1–2 tablespoons of milk whenever the sauce starts to dry out. **5. Place** a large pot of salted water over high heat and bring to a boil. Cook the pasta in the boiling water until al dente, 3–4 minutes. **6. Drain** and arrange on serving plates. Spoon the sauce over the top. **7. Sprinkle** with the Parmesan and serve hot.

Bolognese meat sauce is a classic. There are many variations on the basic recipe; this one is our favorite. Try to cook it for as long as you can; the longer the better. It goes well with almost any pasta type.

● **if you liked this recipe, try the pappardelle with sicilian meat sauce on page 96.**

pappardelle with
sicilian meat sauce

SERVES 4 · PREPARATION 30 MINUTES + TIME TO MAKE THE PASTA · COOKING 55–60 MINUTES

PASTA

14 ounces (400 g) fresh pappardelle,
storebought or homemade (see pages 6–7)

SAUCE

1/4 cup (60 ml) extra-virgin olive oil · 8 ounces (250 g) ground (minced) pork
8 ounces (250 g) round (minced) veal · 2 tablespoons tomato paste (concentrate)
1/2 cup (125 ml) dry white or dry red wine · 1 (14-ounce/400-g) can tomatoes, with juice
Salt and freshly ground black pepper · 3 ounces (90 g) ricotta salata cheese
8 ounces (250 g) fresh ricotta cheese, drained

PASTA   **1. Prepare** the pappardelle following the
instructions on pages 6–7, or use storebought pasta, as
preferred.
SAUCE   **2. Heat** the oil in a large frying pan over medium
heat. Add the pork and veal and sauté until browned, 5–8
minutes. **3. Add** the tomato paste mixed with the wine.
Simmer for 4–5 minutes, then add the tomatoes and
season with salt and pepper. Partially cover the pan
and simmer over low heat for 45 minutes. **4. Place** a
large pot of salted water over high heat and bring to
a boil. Cook the pappardelle in the boiling water
until al dente, 3–4 minutes. **5. While** the pasta is
cooking, use a fork to break the ricotta salata
into small, crumbly pieces. **6. Mix** the fresh ricotta with 2
tablespoons of the cooking water in a large, heated serving
dish. **7. Drain** the pasta and toss carefully with the fresh
ricotta and meat sauce. **8. Sprinkle** with the ricotta salata
and serve hot.

*Ricotta salata is an aged cheese made
from sheep's milk. It is quite salty and full
of flavor so is perfect for sprinkling over
pasta dishes. Use pecorino romano if you
can't find it.*

• **If you liked this recipe**, try the pappardelle with lamb sauce on page 98.

pappardelle with lamb sauce

PASTA

14 ounces (400 g) fresh pappardelle, weighing about 2½ pounds (1.2 kg) · ¼ cup (60 ml) extra-virgin olive oil · 3 tablespoons butter · 1 leg of lamb, storebought or homemade (see pages 6–7)

SAUCE

½ cup (120 ml) Vin Santo or sherry · Salt and freshly ground white pepper · 4 cups (1 liter) beef stock · 1 small onion, finely chopped · 2 tablespoons all-purpose (plain) flour · 1 lettuce heart, cut in strips · 1 tablespoon finely chopped fresh marjoram + extra leaves, to garnish · 6–8 threads saffron, crumbled

SERVES 4 · **PREPARATION** 30 MINUTES + TIME TO MAKE THE PASTA · **COOKING** 2½ HOURS

PASTA 1. Prepare the pappardelle following the instructions on pages 6–7, or use storebought pasta, as preferred. **SAUCE 2. Heat** the oil and butter in a large casserole or saucepan over high heat and sauté the lamb until browned all over, 8–10 minutes. **3. Pour in** the wine and cook until evaporated. Season with salt and pepper. Simmer over low heat until very tender, about 2 hours. Moisten with the stock during cooking. **4. Take** the lamb out of the pan and remove the meat from the bone. Cut the meat into small strips. **5. Add** 3 tablespoons of stock to the pan with the cooking juices. Add the onion and simmer for 5 minutes. **6. Return** the lamb to the pan and simmer for 5 minutes. **7. Stir in** the flour and 2 cups (500 ml) of stock. Add the lettuce, marjoram, and saffron and season with salt and pepper. Simmer over low heat until the lettuce has wilted and the sauce has thickened, about 5 minutes. **8. About** 30 minutes before the sauce is ready, bring a large pan of salted water to a boil over high heat. Cook the pasta until al dente, 3–4 minutes. **9. Drain** well and transfer to a heated serving dish. Spoon the sauce over the top and toss gently. **10. Serve** hot, garnished with the marjoram.

● If you liked this recipe, try the tagliatelle with bolognese meat sauce on page 94.

maltagliati with tomato & sausage sauce

PASTA

1 recipe fresh pasta dough (see page 6)

SAUCE

3 fresh Italian sausages (about 12 ounces/300 g) • 2 tablespoons extra-virgin olive oil • 1 red onion, finely chopped • 3 tablespoons finely chopped fresh parsley • Salt and freshly ground black pepper • 1 pinch ground cinnamon • 1 (14-ounce/400-g) can tomatoes, with juice • 1/2 cup (120) ml dry red wine • 4 tablespoons freshly grated Parmesan cheese

SERVES 4 • **PREPARATION** 15 MINUTES + TIME TO MAKE THE PASTA • **COOKING** 10–12 MINUTES

PASTA 1. Prepare the pasta dough and roll into sheets following the instructions on pages 6–7. **2. Dry** the sheets of pasta on a lightly floured cloth for 30 minutes. **3. Cut** into strips 3/4 inch (2 cm) wide and then into small triangles and squares. **4. Place** a large pot of salted water over high heat and bring to a boil. **SAUCE 5. Prick** the sausages well with a fork then cook for 3 minutes in a pan of boiling water. Drain, peel, and chop coarsely. **6. Heat** the oil in a large frying pan over low heat and sweat the onion and 2 tablespoons of parsley with a pinch of salt for 10 minutes. **7. Add** the sausage meat and sauté over high heat for 5 minutes. **8. Season** with the salt, pepper, and cinnamon. Pour in the wine and cook until evaporated. Add the tomatoes and simmer on low for 20 minutes. **9. Cook** the pasta in the pot of boiling water until al dente, 3–4 minutes. **10. Drain** and add to the pan with the sauce. Toss gently, sprinkle with the Parmesan, and garnish with the remaining parsley. **11. Serve** hot.

Maltagliati means "badly cut" and refers to the haphazard way the pasta is cut up. If you don't have time to make the pasta dough, you can serve this sauce with storebought tagliatelle.

• If you liked this recipe, try spaghetti with meatballs on page 74.

maltagliati with red kidney beans

PASTA

1 recipe fresh pasta dough (see page 6)

FILLING

12 ounces (350 g) dried red kidney or borlotti beans, soaked overnight
8 cups (2 liters) cold water · 4 cloves garlic, 2 whole, 2 finely chopped · 1 bunch
fresh sage · Salt · 2 tablespoons extra-virgin olive oil · 2 tablespoons finely chopped
fresh parsley · 6 tomatoes, diced · Freshly ground black pepper

SERVES 4–6 · **PREPARATION** 1 HOUR + 12 HOURS TO SOAK · **COOKING** 1½ HOURS

PASTA **1. Prepare** the pasta dough and roll into sheets following the instructions on pages 6–7. **2. Dry** the sheets of pasta on a lightly floured cloth for 30 minutes and then into strips 3/4 inch (2 cm) wide and **3. Cut into** small triangles and squares.

SAUCE **4. Put** the beans in a large saucepan with the water, whole garlic cloves, and most of the sage (reserve a few leaves to garnish). Bring to a boil and simmer over low heat until tender, about 1 hour. Season with salt and drain, reserving the water. **5. Heat** the oil in a medium saucepan over

medium heat. Add the finely chopped garlic and parsley and sauté until pale gold, 3–4 minutes. **6. Add** the tomatoes and season with salt and pepper. Simmer for 20 minutes. **7. Add** the beans and a few tablespoons of the cooking water. **8. Place** a large pot of salted water over high heat and bring to a boil. Cook the pasta in the pot of boiling water until al dente, 3–4 minutes. **9. Drain** and divide evenly among four to six serving dishes. **10. Spoon** the sauce over the top and serve hot, garnished with the reserved sage.

This is a hearty and nutritious dish that you can serve as a one-dish meal. It is perfect for vegetarians.

● **if you liked this recipe, try the spaghetti with cincinnati chili on page 76.**

smoked salmon ravioli with lemon & dill sauce

SERVES 4 · PREPARATION 1 HOUR · COOKING 5–10 MINUTES

PASTA
1 recipe fresh pasta dough (see page 8)

FILLING
5 ounces (150 g) smoked salmon · 1 large egg white · 1½ tablespoons light (single) cream · 2 teaspoons coarsely chopped fresh dill

LEMON & DILL SAUCE
1 tablespoon butter · 1 tablespoon all-purpose (plain) flour · ¾ cup (180 ml) dry white wine ¾ cup (180 ml) heavy (double) cream · Freshly squeezed juice of ½ lemon · 2 tablespoons coarsely chopped fresh dill + extra, to garnish · Salt and freshly ground black pepper · Unwaxed lemon zest, to garnish

PASTA **1. Prepare** the pasta dough and roll into sheets following the instructions on pages 6–7. **FILLING** **2. Combine** the salmon, 1 tablespoon of egg white, cream, and dill in a food processor and process until well combined (like a mousse). **3. Prepare** the ravioli with this filling following the instructions on page 10. **Transfer** to a floured cloth until ready to cook. **4. Place** a large pot of salted water over high heat and bring to a boil. Cook the pasta in the boiling water until al dente, 2–3 minutes.

LEMON & DILL SAUCE **5. Melt** the butter in a small saucepan. Add the flour and stir for 1 minute. Turn up the heat. Add the wine, stirring until smooth, followed by the cream and lemon juice. Bring to a boil and simmer until slightly thickened. **6. Add** the dill and season with salt and pepper. **7. Drain** the pasta and divide among four heated serving dishes. **8. Spoon** the sauce over the top, garnish with dill and lemon zest, and serve hot.

The delicate flavor of the smoked salmon filling goes beautifully with the creamy lemon and dill sauce. Serve on special occasions with a glass of chilled white wine.

• If you liked this recipe, try the ricotta ravioli with tomato & zucchini sauce on page 106.

ricotta ravioli with
tomato & zucchini sauce

PASTA

1 recipe fresh pasta dough (see page 6)

FILLING

1 pound (500 g) ricotta cheese · 3/4 cup (90 g) freshly grated pecorino cheese · 1 large egg · 2 tablespoons finely chopped fresh mint

SAUCE

1/4 cup (60 ml) extra-virgin olive oil · 2 cloves garlic, finely chopped · 1 pound (500 g) zucchini (courgettes), cut in matchsticks · 3 tomatoes, peeled and coarsely chopped · 3 tablespoons finely chopped fresh basil + extra leaves, to garnish · Salt and freshly ground black pepper

SERVES 6 · PREPARATION 45 MINUTES + TIME TO REST PASTA · COOKING 20-25 MINUTES

PASTA 1. Prepare the pasta dough and roll into sheets following the instructions on pages 6-7.
FILLING 2. Strain the ricotta into a bowl and mix in the pecorino, egg, and mint. Season with salt and pepper. **3. Put** the filling in a pastry bag fitted with a smooth tip and chill until ready to use. **4. Prepare** the ravioli with this filling following the instructions on page 8. Transfer to a floured cloth until ready to cook. **5. Place** a large pot of salted water over high heat and bring to a boil.

SAUCE 6. Heat the oil in a large frying pan over medium heat. Add the garlic and sauté until it turns pale gold, 3-4 minutes. **7. Add** the zucchini and sauté until tender, about 5 minutes. **8. Add** the tomatoes and basil and simmer for 10 minutes. Season with salt and pepper. **9. Cook** the pasta in the pot of boiling water until al dente, 2-3 minutes. **10. Drain** well and divide evenly among six serving dishes. Spoon the zucchini sauce over the top. **11. Serve** hot, garnishing each dish with the extra basil.

If you are short of time, just make the sauce and serve with 1¼ pounds (600 g) of storebought fresh ricotta ravioli.

● *if you liked this recipe, try the ravioli with ricotta & pecorino on page 108.*

ravioli with ricotta & pecorino

SERVES 4 · PREPARATION 45 MINUTES + TIME TO REST PASTA · COOKING 20 MINUTES

PASTA

1 recipe fresh pasta dough (see page 6)

FILLING

12 ounces (350 g) fresh ricotta cheese, drained · 1/4 cup (60 g) butter
3 tablespoons freshly grated Parmesan cheese · 3 tablespoons beef stock
1 large egg · Pinch of freshly grated nutmeg · Salt and freshly ground white pepper

SAUCE

1/4 cup (60 g) butter · 3 tablespoons beef stock · 3/4 cup (180 ml) heavy (double) cream
3 ounces (90 g) pecorino cheese, in shavings · Freshly parsley, to garnish

PASTA **1. Prepare** the pasta dough and roll into sheets following the instructions on pages 6–7. FILLING **2. Mix** the ricotta, butter, Parmesan, beef stock, egg, nutmeg, salt, and pepper in a bowl. Chill until ready to use. **3. Prepare** the ravioli with this filling following the instructions on page 8. Transfer to a floured cloth until ready to cook. **4. Place** a large pot of salted water over high heat and bring to a boil. SAUCE **5. Melt** the butter with the beef stock in a small saucepan. Simmer for 1–2 minutes. **6. Pour in** the cream and simmer on very low heat for 10 minutes. **7. Cook** the pasta in the pot of boiling water until al dente, 2–3 minutes. **8. Drain** well and divide evenly among four serving dishes. Spoon the sauce over the top. **9. Serve** hot, garnishing each dish with shavings of pecorino and the parsley.

This is the perfect dish for cheese-lovers. Serve with a glass of fine red wine.

● **If you liked this recipe, try the cheese & pear tortelloni on page 112.**

asian ravioli

FILLING

7 ounces (200 g) cabbage, thinly sliced

Salt · 8 ounces (250 g) ground (minced) lean pork

2 tablespoons finely chopped lemon grass · 1 small carrot, finely chopped · 3 scallions (spring onions), finely chopped + extra, to garnish

1 tablespoon soy sauce + extra, to serve · 2 tablespoons sherry · 1 tablespoon cornstarch (cornflour) · 1 teaspoon finely chopped fresh ginger · Pinch of sugar

PASTA

1 cup (150 g) all-purpose (plain) flour · 1/3 cup (50 g) hard (durum) wheat flour · 1 tablespoon peanut oil

About 1/3 cup (90 ml) warm water

SERVES 4 · PREPARATION 45 MINUTES + TIME FOR THE PASTA · COOKING 10 MINUTES

FILLING **1. Put** the cabbage in a large bowl and rub in 2–3 pinches of salt. Set aside for 1 hour. PASTA **2. Prepare** the pasta dough using the ingredients listed here following the instructions on page 8. For this recipe the liquid is provided by the oil and water instead of the egg. Let rest for 30 minutes. **3. Squeeze** the cabbage to remove excess water. Return to the bowl and add the pork, lemon grass, carrot, scallions, soy sauce, sherry, cornstarch, ginger, and sugar. Use your hands to mix well. Refrigerate until ready to use. **4. Divide** the dough into 4 pieces and roll it through the machine one notch at a time down to the thinnest setting. **5. Prepare** the half-moon ravioli following the instructions on page 9. If the pasta is too dry to seal, brush the edges with a little warm water. Transfer the ravioli to a floured cloth until ready to cook. **6. Place** a large

7. **Place** an oriental pasta steamer over the pan. Arrange the ravioli in the steamer, spacing well, and steam for 10 minutes. **8. Serve** hot with extra soy sauce, garnished with scallions.

pot of salted water over high heat and bring to a boil.

These oriental ravioli are a little different from traditional Italian types. Serve them hot with a glass of cold beer.

• If you liked this recipe, try the smoked salmon ravioli with lemon & dill sauce on page 104.

cheese & pear tortelloni

SERVES 4 · PREPARATION 45 MINUTES + TIME FOR THE PASTA · COOKING 10–15 MINUTES

PASTA

1 recipe fresh pasta dough (see page 6)

FILLING

1¼ cups (150 g) coarsely grated pecorino cheese · 5 ounces (150 g) fresh ricotta cheese, drained · 1 small pear, peeled, cored, and coarsely grated

1 large egg · Salt and freshly ground white pepper

SAUCE

4 tablespoons coarsely grated Pecorino cheese · 6 tablespoons (90 g) melted butter

Freshly ground black pepper

PASTA 1. Prepare the pasta dough and roll into sheets following the instructions on pages 6–7. **FILLING 2. Mix** the pecorino, ricotta, pear, egg, salt, and pepper in a medium bowl. Chill until ready to use. **3. Prepare** the tortelloni with this filling following the instructions on page 9. Transfer to a floured cloth until ready to cook. **4. Place** a large pot of salted water over high heat and bring to a boil. Cook the pasta in 2 or 3 batches in the boiling water until al dente, about 3–4 minutes. **5. Scoop out** with a slotted spoon, drain well, and transfer to individual serving dishes. **6. Sprinkle** with the pecorino, drizzle with the butter, and season generously with pepper. **7. Serve** hot.

Tortelloni are the same as the more common tortellini, only larger.

● If you liked this recipe, try the whole-wheat penne with pears & gorgonzola on page 50.

PASTA

1 pound (500 g) storebought tortellini

MEAT SAUCE

1 onion, finely chopped · 1 stalk celery, finely chopped · 1 carrot, finely chopped · 1 stalk celery, finely chopped · 2 tablespoons butter · 12 ounces (350 g) ground (minced) lean pork 8 ounces (250 g) ground (minced) lean beef · 2 Italian sausages, crumbled · 2 chicken livers, coarsely chopped · 1 cup (250 ml) dry red wine · 1 (14-ounce/400 g) can tomatoes Salt and freshly ground black pepper

SERVES 4–6 · **PREPARATION** 15 MINUTES · **COOKING** 2 HOURS

tortellini with
meat sauce

MEAT SAUCE **1. Melt** the butter in a large heavy-bottomed saucepan over medium heat. Add the onion, carrot, and celery and sauté until softened, about 5 minutes. **2. Add** the pork, beef, sausages, and chicken livers; moisten with the wine and cook until it has evaporated. **3. Melt** the tomatoes, salt, and pepper. Cover and leave to simmer gently for 2 hours. Moisten the sauce with a little water if it dries out during cooking. PASTA **4. Place** a large pot of salted water over high heat and bring to a boil. Cook the pasta in the boiling water until al dente, 3–5 minutes. **5. Drain** well and transfer to a heated serving dish. Spoon the sauce over the top and toss gently. **6. Serve** hot.

Tortellini are a classic stuffed pasta from Bologna, in central Italy.

• If you liked this recipe, try the cheese & pear tortelloni on page 112.

114

classic lasagna

SERVES 6 · PREPARATION 1 HOUR · COOKING 2½ HOURS

PASTA

1 recipe fresh pasta dough (see page 6)

MEAT SAUCE

⅓ cup (90 g) butter · 8 ounces (250 g) prosciutto, finely chopped
1 onion, finely chopped · 1 carrot, finely chopped · 1 stalk celery, finely
chopped · 12 ounces (350 g) ground (minced) beef · ⅓ cup (90 ml) dry white wine
1 large tomato, peeled and chopped · ½ cup (120 ml) beef stock · Salt · 1¼ cups
(150 g) freshly grated Parmesan · 2 tablespoons butter

BÉCHAMEL SAUCE

1 recipe Béchamel sauce (see page 118)

MEAT SAUCE **1. Melt** the butter in a medium saucepan over medium heat. Add the prosciutto, onion, carrot, and celery. Sauté until the vegetables have softened, about 5 minutes. **2. Add** the beef and sauté until lightly browned, about 5 minutes. **3. Pour** in the wine and simmer until evaporated. Add the tomato and stock. Mix well and season with salt. Cover and simmer over low heat for 2 hours. Stir the sauce from time to time and add a little more stock if it begins to stick to the pan. PASTA **4. Prepare** the pasta dough following the instructions on pages 6. **5. Prepare** and blanch the lasagna sheets following the instructions on page 11. **6. Preheat** the oven to 400°F (200°C/gas 6). **7. Butter** an ovenproof dish measuring about 8 x 12 inches (20 x 30 cm). **8. Line** the prepared baking dish with a layer of pasta. Cover with a layer of Béchamel, meat sauce, and Parmesan. Top with a layer of pasta. Repeat these layers until all the ingredients are in the dish. Sprinkle with the remaining Parmesan and dot with the remaining butter. **9. Bake** until golden brown and bubbling, about 20 minutes. **10. Serve** hot. Let rest for 10 minutes.

• If you liked this recipe, try the pesto lasagna on page 118.

116

PASTA

1 recipe fresh pasta dough (see page 6)
2 tablespoons extra-virgin olive oil

BÉCHAMEL SAUCE

5 tablespoons (75 g) butter · ¹/₂ cup (75 g) all-purpose (plain) flour · Pinch of
freshly grated nutmeg · 4 cups (1 liter) milk · Salt and freshly ground white pepper

PESTO

3–4 bunches basil (with small leaves) · 1 clove garlic · ³/₄ cup (90 g) freshly grated Parmesan cheese
2 tablespoons freshly grated pecorino cheese · 2 walnuts, shelled · 3 tablespoons pine nuts
³/₄ cup (180 ml) extra-virgin olive oil · 1 teaspoon coarse sea salt

SERVES 6 · **PREPARATION** 1 HOUR · **COOKING** 40 MINUTES

pesto **lasagna**

PASTA **1. Prepare** the pasta dough following the instructions on pages 6. **2. Prepare** and blanch the lasagna sheets following the instructions on page 11. **3. Preheat** the oven to 400°F (200°C/gas 6). **4. Butter** an ovenproof dish measuring about 8 x 12 inches (20 x 30 cm).

BÉCHAMEL SAUCE **5. Melt** the butter in a medium saucepan over medium heat, then stir in the flour and nutmeg. Cook for 1–2 minutes, stirring constantly, then add the milk all at once. Season with salt and pepper. Bring to a boil, stirring constantly. Simmer until thick, stirring constantly, 5–10 minutes.

PESTO **6. Combine** the basil, garlic, 2 tablespoons of Parmesan, the pecorino, walnuts, pine nuts, oil, and salt in a food processor and chop until smooth and creamy. **7. Line** the prepared baking dish with a layer of pasta. Cover with a layer of Béchamel, pesto, and Parmesan. Top with a layer of pasta. Repeat these layers until all the ingredients are in the dish. **8. Bake** for 20 minutes, until a light crust has formed on the top. **9. Let stand** for 10 minutes before serving.

This is a delicious alternative to classic lasagna, which is made with meat sauce.

● If you liked this recipe, try the classic lasagna on page 116.

potato gnocchi with butter & sage

SERVES 6–8 • **PREPARATION** 10 MINUTES + TIME TO MAKE THE GNOCCHI • **COOKING** 10 MINUTES

GNOCCHI

1 recipe potato gnocchi (see page 10)
or 2 pounds (1 kg) storebought potato gnocchi

SAUCE

½ cup (120 g) butter • 16–20 leaves fresh sage
• 1 cup (120 g) freshly grated Parmesan cheese

GNOCCHI **1. Prepare** the gnocchi following the instructions on page 10, or use storebought gnocchi, as preferred. **2. Place** a large pot of salted water over high heat and bring to a boil. **3. Cook** the gnocchi in batches. Lower the first batch (20–24 gnocchi) gently into the boiling water. After a few minutes they will rise to the surface. Scoop out with a slotted spoon. **4. Divide** the cooked gnocchi equally among six to eight serving dishes. Repeat until all the gnocchi are cooked. SAUCE **5. Melt** the butter with the sage in a small saucepan over low heat. Simmer until the butter is just beginning to color, 1–2 minutes. **6. Drizzle** over the gnocchi. **7. Sprinkle** with the Parmesan and serve hot.

Fresh, homemade potato gnocchi are so much better than the rubbery concoctions often available in supermarkets. Their delicate flavor requires nothing more than this toasted butter and sage sauce.

• If you liked this recipe, try the potato gnocchi with tomato sauce on page 122.

120

potato gnocchi
with tomato sauce

GNOCCHI

1 recipe potato gnocchi (see page 10)
or 2 pounds (1 kg) storebought potato gnocchi)

TOMATO SAUCE

3 tablespoons extra-virgin olive oil · 1 onion, finely chopped · 2 pounds (1 kg)
tomatoes, peeled, or 2 (14-ounce/400-g) cans tomatoes, with juice · 2 tablespoons
coarsely chopped fresh basil + extra leaves, to garnish · Salt and freshly ground black pepper
½ cup (60 g) freshly grated Parmesan cheese

SERVES 6–8 · **PREPARATION** 20 MINUTES + TIME FOR THE GNOCCHI · **COOKING** 30–40 MINUTES

GNOCCHI 1. Prepare the gnocchi following the instructions on page 10, or use storebought gnocchi, as preferred. **TOMATO SAUCE 2. Heat** the oil in a large frying pan over medium heat. Add the onion and sauté until softened, 3–4 minutes. **3. Add** the tomatoes and basil and season with salt and pepper. Simmer over low heat until reduced, 15–20 minutes. **4. Place** a large pot of salted water over high heat and bring to a boil. **5. Cook** the gnocchi in batches. Lower the first batch (20–24 gnocchi) gently into the boiling water. After a few minutes they will rise to the surface. Scoop out with a slotted spoon. **6. Divide** the cooked gnocchi equally among six to eight serving dishes. Repeat until all the gnocchi are cooked. **7. Spoon** some tomato sauce over each serving. **8. Sprinkle** with Parmesan, garnish with basil, and serve hot.

Potato gnocchi go very well with tomato sauce but they are also good with many other sauces in this book. Try them with pesto (see page 28), walnut pesto (see page 32), and Bolognese meat sauce (see page 94).

● If you liked this recipe, try the potato gnocchi with butter & sage on page 120.

spinach gnocchi with tomato sauce

SERVES *4–6* · **PREPARATION** 1 HOUR + TIME FOR THE SAUCE · **COOKING** 10–15 MINUTES

GNOCCHI

1 pound (500 g) fresh ricotta, strained through a fine-mesh sieve · 1½ cups (350 g) finely chopped cooked spinach, well drained · 2 large eggs · 1 cup (120 g) freshly grated Parmesan cheese + extra, to serve · ½ cup (75 g) + 2 tablespoons all-purpose (plain) flour · Salt and freshly ground black pepper · Finely grated zest of ½ unwaxed lemon

TOMATO SAUCE

1 recipe tomato sauce (see page 122)

GNOCCHI 1. Mix the ricotta and spinach in a large bowl. Add the eggs, Parmesan, and ½ cup (75 g) of flour. Season with salt and pepper and add the lemon zest. **2. Dip** your hands in the remaining 2 tablespoons of flour and form the spinach mixture into 2-inch (5-cm) balls. Set aside on a floured cloth until ready to serve. **3. Place** a large pot of salted water over high heat and bring to a boil. **4. Cook** the gnocchi in batches. Lower the first batch (20–24 gnocchi) gently into the boiling water. After a few minutes they will rise to the surface. Scoop out with a slotted spoon. **5. Divide** the gnocchi equally among four to six serving dishes. Repeat until all the gnocchi are cooked. **6. Spoon** tomato sauce over each serving and sprinkle with Parmesan. **7. Serve** hot.

These gnocchi come from Tuscany where they are known as "gnudi," (naked), because they are like the spinach and ricotta filling for Tuscan ravioli without their pasta coverings. They are not especially difficult to make and are always delicious. You can serve with this tomato sauce, or just use a simple butter and herb sauce (like the one we used on page 120 for potato gnocchi).

• If you liked this recipe, try the potato & carrot gnocchi with arugula pesto on page 126.

potato & carrot gnocchi
with arugula pesto

GNOCCHI
2 pounds (1 kg) carrots, sliced · 1 pound (500 g) potatoes, peeled and cut into chunks · 1 large egg, lightly beaten · 1⅓ cups (200 g) all-purpose (plain) flour · Salt and freshly ground white pepper · ¼ teaspoon freshly grated nutmeg

ARUGULA PESTO
2 cups (100 g) arugula (rocket) · 2 cloves garlic · 4 tablespoons pine nuts · ⅔ cup (100 g) freshly grated pecorino cheese · Salt and freshly ground black pepper · ½ cup (120 ml) extra-virgin olive oil

SERVES 6–8 · **PREPARATION** 15 MINUTES + 1–2 HOURS TO DRY · **COOKING** 25–35 MINUTES

GNOCCHI **1. Cook** the carrots and potatoes in a large pot of boiling water until tender, 15–20 minutes. Drain well. **2. Mash** the carrots and potatoes together and let cool a little. **3. Stir in** the egg, flour, salt, white pepper, and nutmeg, mixing well with a wooden spoon to make a firm dough. **4. Working quickly,** scoop out pieces of dough and roll them on a lightly floured work surface into long sausage shapes about ¾ inch (2 cm) in diameter. Cut the sausage shapes into pieces about 1 inch (2.5 cm) long. **5. Set** the gnocchi out on a floured clean cloth, making sure that they don't touch, and leave for 1–2 hours to dry.

ARUGULA PESTO **6. Combine** the arugula, garlic, pine nuts, cheese, salt, and pepper in a food processor and process until finely chopped. With the motor running, gradually add the oil. **7. Place** a large pot of salted water over high heat and bring to a boil. **8. Cook** the gnocchi in batches. Lower the first batch (20–24 gnocchi) gently into the boiling water. After a few minutes they will rise to the surface. Scoop out with a slotted spoon. **9. Divide** the gnocchi equally among six to eight serving dishes. Repeat until all the gnocchi are cooked. **10. Spoon** the arugula pesto over the gnocchi, tossing gently. **11. Serve** hot.

● If you liked this recipe, try the spinach gnocchi with tomato sauce on page 124.

126

index

Asian ravioli 110
Bucatini all'Amatriciana 20
Bucatini alla carbonara 18
Bucatini with leek & tomato
sauce 38

Cavatappi with spicy tomato
sauce 42
Cavatelli with pancetta &
tomato sauce 78
Cheese & pear tortelloni 112
Classic lasagna 116
Conchiglie salad with blue
cheese & apples 40

Farfalle salad with cherry
tomatoes & feta 30
Farfalle with tuna & olives 58
Fusilli with gorgonzola
& peas 22
Fusilli with sun-dried tomato
& ricotta pesto 26

Linguine with mussels 70
Linguine with pesto, beans
& potatoes 28
Linguine with tomatoes
& clams 62

Linguine with tomatoes
& lemon 14
Linguine with walnut pesto 32

Maltagliati with tomato
beans 102
Maltagliati with tomato
& sausage sauce 100

Orecchiette with broccoli 80

Pappardelle with lamb
sauce 98
Pappardelle with Sicilian meat
sauce 96
Penne with grilled summer
veggies 36
Penne with tomatoes
& mozzarella 16
Pesto lasagna 118
Potato & carrot gnocchi
with arugula pesto 126
Potato gnocchi with butter
& sage 120
Potato gnocchi with tomato
sauce 122

Ravioli with ricotta
& pecorino 108

Ricotta ravioli with tomato
& zucchini sauce 106
Rigatoni with tomatoes
& goat cheese 44
Rigatoni with tomatoes,
ricotta & pesto 48
Ruote with shrimp
& zucchini 66

Smoked salmon ravioli
with lemon & dill
sauce 104
Spaghetti alla puttanesca 24
Spaghetti with Cincinnati
chili 76
Spaghetti with clams
& arugula 64
Spaghetti with garlic, chile
& oil 12
Spaghetti with meatballs 74
Spaghetti with Mediterranean
pesto 46
Spaghetti with seafood
al cartoccio 72
Spaghetti with squid ink 60
Spaghettini with crab
& lemon 68
Spicy spaghetti with pancetta
& onion 56

Spicy tagliatelle with eggplant
sauce 86
Spinach gnocchi with tomato
sauce 124

Tagliatelle Caprese 88
Tagliatelle with Bolognese
meat sauce 94
Tagliatelle with salmon, cream
& peas 90
Tagliatelle with scallops
& bread crumbs 92
Tagliolini with mascarpone
& eggs 82
Tortellini with meat sauce 114

Watercress tagliolini
with pesto 84
Whole-wheat fusilli with
veggies, feta & herbs 34
Whole-wheat penne with
pears & gorgonzola 50
Whole-wheat spaghetti
with pancetta & bell
peppers 52
Whole-wheat spaghetti
with spicy anchovy sauce 54

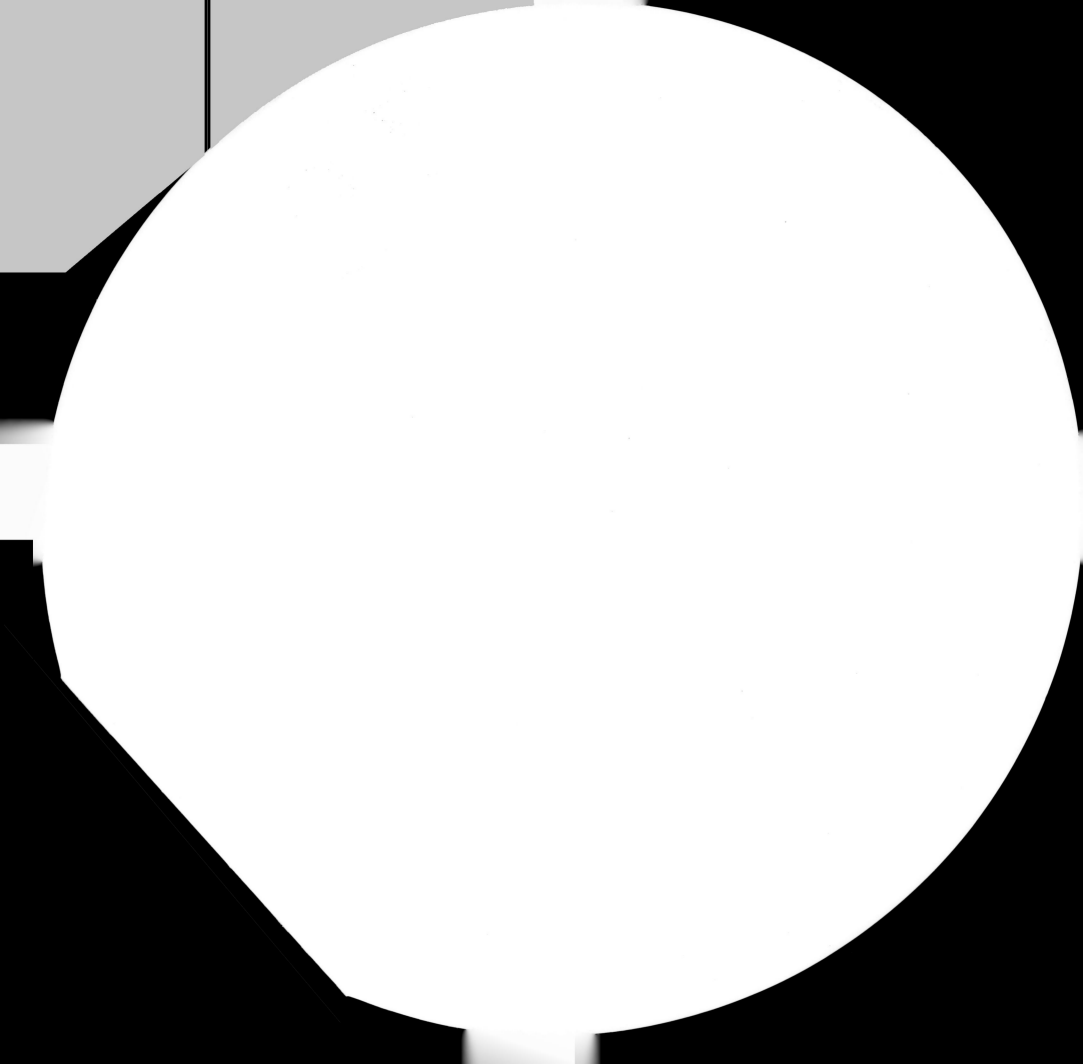

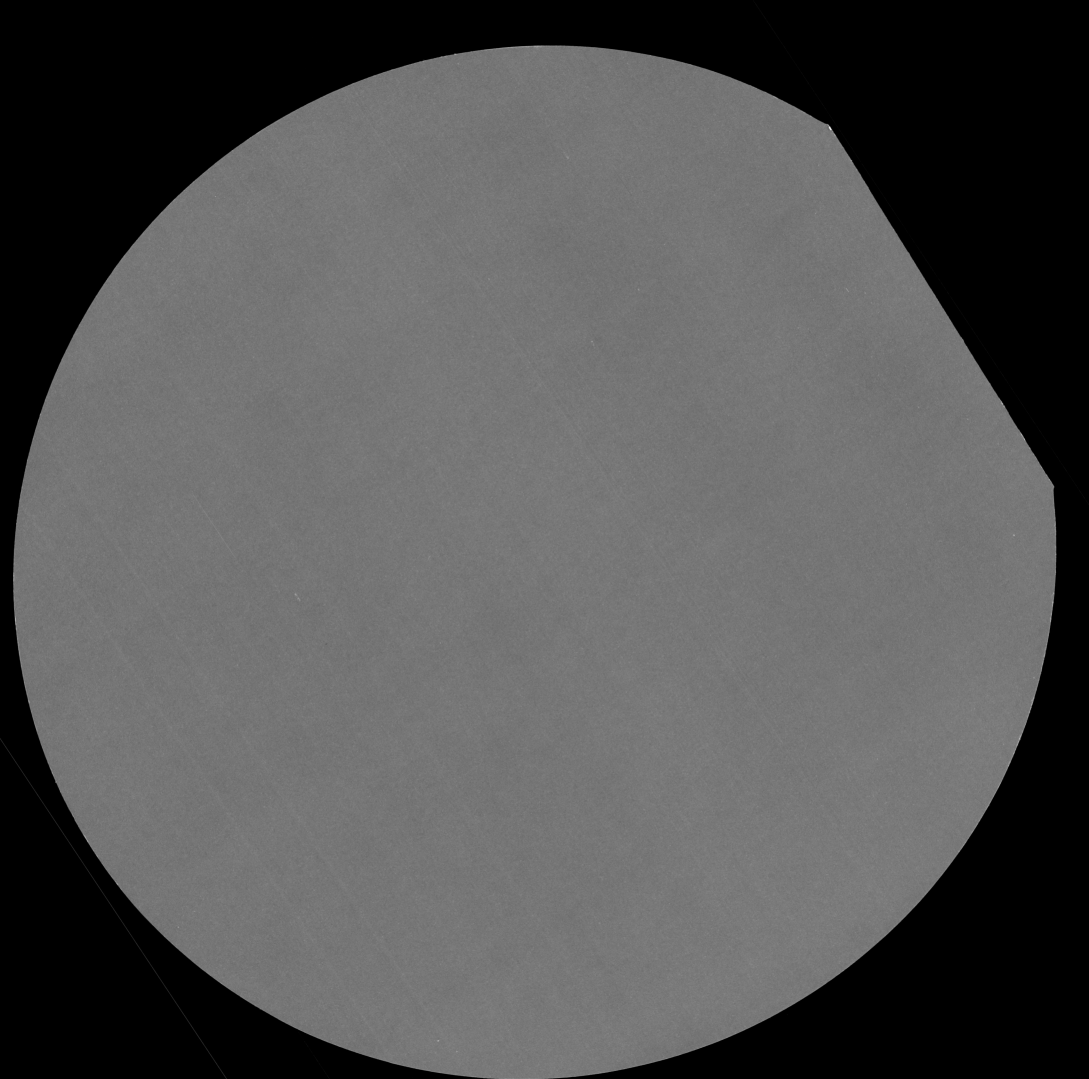